*f*P

Also by David Gelernter

The Muse in the Machine: Computerizing the Poetry
of Human Thought
1939: The Lost World of the Fair

DRAWING
LIFE

*Surviving
the Unabomber*

David Gelernter

THE FREE PRESS

New York   London   Toronto   Sydney   Singapore

THE FREE PRESS
A Division of Simon & Schuster Inc.
1230 Avenue of the Americas
New York, NY 10020

Manufactured in the United States of America

10   9   8   7   6   5   4   3   2   1

Library of Congress Cataloging-in-Publication Data

Gelernter, David Hillel.
    Drawing life : surviving the Unabomber / David Gelernter.
    p.   cm.
    ISBN 0-684-83912-1
    1. Gelernter, David Hillel.   2. Victims of terrorism—United
States—Biography.   3. Bombings—United States.   I. Title.
HV6432.G45A3   1997
364.15'23'092—dc21
    [B]   97-13190
                                                                  CIP

viii

159

For my parents
and my Jane

ACKNOWLEDGMENTS

M<small>ANY PEOPLE</small> helped my wife and me get through the episode this book describes; some are mentioned in a book I published in 1994, but I would like to re-thank them here because this book is about the bomb story and that one wasn't.

Thanks are due first to our families: to my brother and his wife, my parents and Jane's parents, Jane's brother Ed and my sister, and our devoted friend Soledad Morales. We couldn't have got through it without them.

The Bialeks and Clemans, Rabbi and Mrs. Benjamin Scolnic, the Agins, the Schwartzes, the Patkins and the Larrisons put themselves out for us repeatedly and helped us, especially with our children. We will always be grateful to them. Jane Milberg and Bob King, the Lermans and Susan Shapiro and (among my colleagues at work) Nick Carriero and Chris Hatchell, Martin and Beverly Schultz and Ed Keegan were indispensable. Among the medical people who worked hard to reassamble me, I am particularly grateful to Rhonda Laidlaw, Marsha Dymarczyk and Drs. Henry Spinelli, Peter Gloor and Joseph Caprioli.

In the normal-acknowledgments category, my thanks once again to my long-suffering editor Susan Arellano and to the whole distinguished cast at The Free Press. An earlier version of parts of this book appeared in *Commentary*, and the whole book has gained greatly from Neal Kozodoy's thoughtful comments.

And of course to my wife Jane, of whom Goethe wrote *ein Blick von dir, ein Wort mehr unterhält/Als alle Weisheit diser Welt*, and of whom *Shir ha'Shirim* said *har'ini et mar'ayich, hashmi'im et koleich, ki koleich areiv u'mar'ayich naveh.*

DRAWING

LIFE

A CHILD NAMED Sigmund Spaeth once published a poem about the first spring of the twentieth century. I wish I could find it. It appeared in *St. Nicholas Magazine,* which used to award prizes for the best poems, essays, drawings and whatnot of American children. The winners were published monthly for an earnest but good-natured child readership; the magazine nuzzles you like an affectionate hound. ("I mean to try the competition every month," writes new subscriber Katherine S. Hazeltine, "but even if I don't get a prize, I am *not* going to be discouraged." "Here is a member with the right spirit" reads the little headline above her letter.)

E. B. White mentions young Sigmund's poem in one of his essays, and not long ago I set off to locate it, invading a corner of the Yale library where evidently no one had been since around 1946. When I found the place and snapped on the light, an aisleful of dignified old books drew itself up in annoyance. But it seems to me that a great library by definition includes places where no one ever goes. And I have always wished to visit the locked and hidden under-the-dome room at Monticello, the Statue of Liberty's torch (you can get there, I am told, by climbing a fenced-off stairway up the raised arm), the forbidden galleries that ring the dome's interior near the top of the Capitol. The great Gothic cathedrals have tower rooms and sub-basements and hidden galleries that a man of my bizarre tastes would pay a lot to get into. A natural wilderness is just a wilderness. A man-made wilderness accumulates history and a special exalted grade of silence. So I love standing in Sterling Library's least-popular aisles like a child alone in fresh snow, but without the frozen ears and wet feet. Libraries have it over nature in many ways.

I searched every *St. Nicholas* in the vicinity of the turn of the century, in vain. I did find some related pieces; they all agree that the twentieth was scheduled to be a wonderful century, the best ever. They are unbearably sad.

One morning in June 1993 I was almost killed by a mail bomb. The FBI arrived that same sunny day to comb through the wreckage of my office as I lay on an operating table and surgeons struggled to reassemble me. A man who has been blown up by a bomb is a mess, and it's much harder to put things back together than smash them up: a truism, but important, and a theme of this story. My office was a mess too—the blast drove shrapnel through steel file cabinets and started a fire, but even before the sprinklers triggered, soaking books, journals, papers and computers, this tableau was an unlikely candidate for the cover of *House Beautiful,* barring an exceptionally slow month in the interior decorator business.

The FBI needed to sift the evidence in hopes of catching the criminal, as eventually it did. From my point of view the twentieth century is the crime scene, and I found as I struggled to regain my balance and get my bearings that I needed to hunt through it. The United States today is vastly richer and stronger than it was when Sigmund wrote that poem; much healthier, more comfortable, longer-lived—and far more violent. Do you doubt that we have made progress? Back in the old days "every other grave," according to E. B. White again in a different context, "was a child's grave." What made crime get so much worse as life got so much better?

Whatever Sigmund wrote, I think I know what his first reaction to modern terrorism would have been: It would have been astonishment. That a man would mail bombs in packages to people he has never met, to hurt and kill indiscriminately while he hides, is above all *surprising*, astonishingly low. But you will find no trace of astonishment in the news stories. (A bomb went off at the 1996 Atlanta Olympics. "The most common response from the public," according to the *Wall Street Journal*, "was one of getting on with business.") My guess is that terrorism bloomed exactly when we were prepared to find it no longer surprising. In the late 1960s (though the roots admittedly reach back earlier), a group of intellectuals entered the freightyard control room and toyed like children with the switches, resetting them for fun—unaware of what they were doing, except making trouble; then the excitement wore off and they slunk away. The trains started to collide before they had even gone, and are still smashing up. This is no issue of Left against Right, it goes deeper, as I will explain—and, yes, it was all a long time ago, but things that are quickly smashed can take a long time to fix. The blast that injured me was a reenactment of a far bigger one a generation earlier, which destroyed something basic in this society that has yet to be repaired. We pretend not to see it.

And yet, although I was hurt permanently and will never get back a normal right hand or right eye—although my chest will always look like a gouged-out construction site—here is the main thing: I recovered. In some ways I am better than before. The nation can recover too. As for my office, I was supposed to move into a new one anyway, and merely went out with a bang. When I made my first tentative appearance back at work in mid-fall, I discovered that my graduate students, together with my talented assistant and devoted friend Chris Hatchell, had set up the new office, in an operation masterminded by a close friend and colleague who plays a starring role in this story: Nick Carriero. The salvage crew had combed through the junk heap of my possessions and pulled survivors out of the wreckage. Then they lugged the whole lot to the new office and put every book and journal on a shelf, every overhead-projector slide (there were millions) in a folder, every notebook and loose paper in a box—each folder meticulously labeled, the books organized by topic, the journals chronological. The whole place was in such an exalted state of order that it was dazzling, and you practically needed sunglasses to look at it. No office of mine had ever been a tenth as neat or (of course) would ever be again. I am no sentimentalist, but the point is too important to pass over and is another of my themes: If you insert into this weird slot machine of modern life one evil act, a thousand acts of kindness tumble out.

We had just gotten back from a vacation in Washington, where the museums and carousel on the Mall turn the tourist-packed downtown into a giant amusement park. Naturally mail accumulates when I'm away, and my assistant had stacked most of it on my desk and put a package on my chair. It looked like a dissertation, I remember thinking; I didn't recognize the name in the return address, but newly graduated Ph.D.'s are always sending their dissertations around. As a rule these are not particularly welcome and are quickly consigned to a "nonurgent reading" pile—"nonurgent" meaning "before hell freezes over, circumstances permitting"—but despite being invariably unpromising, they rarely actually explode.

It was a book package with a plastic zip cord. When I pulled the cord acrid white smoke billowed out—I remember the hiss and the strange smell—and moments later, a terrific flash. My first thought was along the lines of: bombs must be going off all over campus this morning. It is a strange thought, but I assumed that I had to be part of a large-scale event. It didn't occur to me that I could possibly have been singled out as a target. I was not in a murder-prone line of work; I had no personal enemies, on account not of being lovable but of being obscure. That very morning, my wife told me later, she'd heard New York Senator Al d'Amato on the radio talking about a death threat he'd gotten—he was peeved—and she had reflected that it was good *we* had nothing to do with politics. Just a quick, thankful thought of a type you would ordinarily never recall.

I couldn't see out of my right eye, and my first thought was that I ought to wash it out, because it might have been sprayed with something that could destroy it. I traipsed to the bathroom in the middle of the building, thinking as I went that a certain graduate student—his office was midway down the hall—usually came in early, and I could get him to call the police; but his office was dark, so I figured I had better call them myself. It hit me as I entered the bathroom that I was bleeding buckets and should come up with another plan. The university health clinic was nearby, up a short rise and across the street to the rear of our building. I spent only a moment in the bathroom, went to the stairs at the front corner of the building and—breathing with difficulty, in pain and royally annoyed—made my way down the five and a half stories to level ground.

FBI men told me later that they had found a shoe in my office and my shirt on the staircase. They asked whether I had torn off the shirt to rig a tourniquet. Possibly, but I don't remember. My recollections feel continuous, but it turns out they are not.

A person's first impulse when he is faced with this sort of thing is to try to fit it into the ordinary events of the day: "You have just, out of the blue, been gravely hurt and all bets are off" is a message the mind doesn't want to hear. By the time I made it outside I understood I was in bad shape, maybe dying, but was still not absolutely clear on whether I would have to cancel my appointments for the *whole* day. When I woke up after surgery and saw my wife hours later, my first thought was: Did they *have* to go bother her? I'd rather have called her myself and de-emphasized the more alarming aspects. I knew at the same time that my condition was critical. That's what the hospital reported, and it certainly felt that way. The mind is like a bottle of salad dressing, capable of operating in mutually incompatible layers.

They told me later that my blood pressure when I arrived at the clinic across the street measured zero; that it was lucky I had decided to walk and not wait for a ride, because I would likely have bled to death otherwise. But it was a very difficult walk. When I looked down at my right hand I saw the bones sticking out in all directions and the skin crumpled like paper.

It could only have been a two- or three-minute walk at the outside, but the possibility existed that I would pass out or keel over or just stop, and I didn't want to. Providentially an old

Zionist marching song with a good strong beat came into my head. Music is valuable. I learned again and again that the old pep-talk folk wisdom we are no longer confident enough to teach our children is *right,* at least much of the time. Months later, when I was home again and feeling bad, Beethoven bore me up. And that Zionist folk song bore me along. As soon as it came to mind, I thought of something else too—a few weeks earlier I had been in Israel. A colleague's father had driven me around the hills outside Jerusalem and reminisced about fighting there during the War of Independence. In Jerusalem the Jewish garrison had been all but cut off; every supply convoy was a bloody struggle. He was a wry, scholarly, peaceful man, the farthest thing from a stereotype soldier. But when fighters were needed, he fought. And the recollection (in the fleeting shape of a night scene in a dark car in the hills) inspired me and helped me stay cogent. History is inspiring. Bravery is inspiring. It is shameful that we no longer teach this to our children.

I pushed through the heavy glass doors of the infirmary and round the corner to the walk-in clinic; I was reeling, but a stretcher materialized under me and people came fast. It was hard to talk, but I managed to tell someone my name and that a mail bomb had done the damage. In the background someone was upbraiding someone else: "You shouldn't have taken him *here.* We're not equipped for it." I managed to put in that I had walked over myself, which caused a brief puzzled silence. Here is a man, they were doubtless thinking, who positively is in no shape for a walk. They didn't know I had only come from computer science, and it didn't occur to me to elaborate, and perhaps they imagined a weird bloody procession through the streets of New Haven with the walker falling apart like a cartoon jalopy. But if they were puzzled, the show kept right on anyway, fast and purposeful; maybe everything is all right after all, I thought, somewhat detached from reality as usual. These people know what they're doing. A mere couple of minutes later a voice behind me said, "We're gonna roll," and they pushed me out to the ambulance at the curb. I didn't picture how long it would be until I would walk another step under my own steam—which, Lord knows, was just as well.

And so I wound up in Yale–New Haven hospital. I don't remember much about the ambulance ride, but recall being rolled on a wheeled carrier under a massive rack of operating-room lights and watching them come on. My last time in an operating room I had been a child in the early 1960s, and removing children's tonsils was a national craze, like the twist. Probably half the doctors in the country did it full time. My parents were against the craze, but they shopped me around to a large number of doctors and each one was positive the tonsils had to go.

Ether was still the anesthetic of choice; you inhaled it (the smell is sickening) and quickly dropped off. But on my return home I got a New York Yankees baseball outfit to cheer me up. Even better, I got to stay home from school and lie on the living room sofa complaining, which is an activity I have always enjoyed—have indeed worked up into an area of expertise. A neighbor brought me a Doctor Kildare jigsaw puzzle. I have difficulty even being in the same room with a jigsaw puzzle, jigsaw-puzzle assembly being an activity designed on purpose to be pointless. Why even *bother* with a puzzle when you can perfectly well spend all day ripping newspapers to bits and taping them back together, if that's the sort of thing that appeals to you?

But I probably managed a weak smile. At least I hope I did. It was awfully nice of her to bring it over.

"I was trying to decide whether to get Ben Casey or Doctor Kildare," she said, perched on the sofa beside me, "but I figured, *Ben Casey* . . ." And her sentence trailed off in scorn. I have always remembered it because I found the logic so utterly impenetrable. I remember thinking something like: What kind of argument is *that?* What's *wrong* with Ben Casey? It's never a good idea to say anything to a child who is destined to be a writer, because (obsessed with language as he is) he will chew it over for conceivably thirty-odd years and then analyze it in a memoir. I still don't understand what made Dr. Kildare such an obvious choice.

CHAPTER TWO

WHEN YOU ARE trying to figure out how a society thinks and feels, words are the surest route to the truth. In recent years we have gotten the habit of using "judgmental" as a pejorative. My beloved 1953 *Webster's Second International* has never heard of the word, nor has my 1969 *American Heritage Dictionary*, nor the 1971 *Oxford English Dictionary*; in the 1993 *Oxford Shorter* there it is at last, smirking.

Some recent book is good, a newspaper review says, because it offers "a kinder, less judgmental explanation" of debt. Another book discusses many a topic that "a less generous writer might well be judgmental about." A character in a play condemns some "ugly judgmental society" or other; a different show includes "an abrasive and judgmental aunt." A benign coach isn't "going to be excessively judgmental," he reassures a reporter, about a player who took money he wasn't supposed to. "Did you see things in South Africa," a returned traveler is asked by another reporter, "that were so different from here in the United States that you had to remind yourself not to be judgmental?" A woman who doesn't want children "had to listen to so much judgmental nonsense on it" that she stopped listening; a deceased dance teacher was terrific insofar as "he was not at all judgmental about whether you got it right or whether it was art." And so on. These examples are all culled at random from American newspapers in the summer of '96. There are lots more where they came from.

This "judgmental" business starts to matter when you have joined it to the other piece of the photo and taped the two halves back together.

O.J. Simpson is widely agreed to be a brutal murderer, and we let him walk. In 1992, the confessed killer of Yankel Rosenbaum was acquitted in state court and convicted at last, five years later, on federal civil rights charges. In a remarkable piece in *The New Republic,* Robyn Gearey writes about the September 1996 murder of a man named Chet Levitt in Washington, D.C. The police interviewed the single witness and then lost track of her. Chances are the case will never be solved; the Washington police, Gearey writes, "don't seem to care much any more about murder." And she backs up this remarkable claim with facts and figures. Maybe there is something exceptional about these cases? Judge Harold Rothwax lays out, in a 1996 book called *Guilty: The Collapse of Criminal Justice,* exactly what constitutes "routine," exactly what happens daily in obscure criminal cases where no one gives a damn, except maybe the victims' grieving relatives. Plea bargains and complex, whimsical exclusionary rules are routine, and criminals routinely go free, every day the court sits, no exceptions. Roughly half the murder cases in Los Angeles yield indictments, and the other half yield nothing, not even a show of justice. In Washington, D.C., around 30 percent of murder cases yield indictments.

Is there any connection between our constantly ordering one another not to be judgmental and our not *being* judgmental? Surely not; surely there couldn't be. After all, a society whose citizens actually were *not* judgmental would be a society without justice.

Later generations will have no trouble picking us out from among the milling throngs: We are the age that was haunted by injustice, by violence and by citizens constantly nagging one another not to be "judgmental." "If thought corrupts language," George Orwell wrote in *Politics and the English Language,* "language also corrupts thought."

As a society we once bristled with contempt for violent criminals. Today we are just as keen as ever to put criminals in jail and make our lives safe from violence. But when we condemn criminals there is rarely any force in our words, only a certain wistful sadness.

When I woke up in the hospital I was surprised to see my wife, annoyed (as I say) that they had gone and told her and happy she was there; she was by my side nearly every waking moment until I left the hospital six weeks later. There was a breathing tube in my mouth, so I couldn't talk, and I was moored with a dozen lines like a rocket fueling for blastoff. A breathing tube creates what must be close to the worst sensation there is. You feel that you are in a permanent state of choking. I was awfully thirsty and had no way to tell anyone; I outlined letter by letter the word "Coke" on a nurse's palm, and this was taken to be in the nature of a great crack—"Ha, his sense of humor survived!"—but "Coke" was merely the shortest way I could think of to convey thirst. The joke was on me; obviously you can't drink when you are breathing through a damned tube. As an extra bonus the table on which I awoke rocked constantly back and forth and side to side. My right lung had been damaged, and the oscillations were supposed to keep it from getting worse. Imagine coming to in a state of acute discomfort, stupefying confusion and general unhappiness atop a gyrating ironing board. And on top of *that* someone announced that Governor Weicker had dropped by. Just the man I wanted to see at this moment, the father of the Connecticut state income tax. But he didn't actually put in a bedside appearance, or possibly he had already left. Politicians are drawn to the targets of showy crimes like fruit flies to ripe bananas. They can't help themselves and probably don't even know they are doing it.

Naturally I had no clear idea of the extent of my injuries. An optimist assumes that, however bad things look in the short term, they will be patched together eventually. Although I should have inferred it from what I had seen, I was surprised and unhappy to learn that the damage to my right hand was permanent, both sides lopped off forever, thumb and little finger, and the middle fingers badly mangled. The plan was in fact to amputate most of the arm, an arm without a hand being useless—it would just get in the way, the surgeon pointed out crisply; but he was planning a last-ditch salvage maneuver to attempt patching up what was left of the hand. If the attempt worked I would have one good hand and one "helper" hand. He was pleased with the plan, but I was unthrilled and less appreciative than I should have been. I didn't see what the hell a man would want with a "helper" hand, had just that morning left home with two real ones and wished the table would stop gyrating.

I am not always the world's most cheerful person to begin with. I am capable of dissolving into deep gloom over (say) my inability to locate last month's *Commentary* magazine, which is probably stashed beneath twenty thousand books and newspapers, slowly turning into sedimentary rock; when my wife asks me what's wrong, she's accustomed to my roaring things like, "Haven't you *seen* what the Whitney is planning for the next Biennial?" I am not incapable of crankiness. I was not cheerful on the hellish gyrating table. But a couple of days later in an all-day operation Dr. Henry Spinelli brought off the daring salvage maneuver, and I will always be grateful to him for having the skill and imagination to do it, however unimpressed I was at the time.

I am hazy about much of my first week in the hospital. I went through two big operations that week, and it takes a while to snap back to normal after a long period of outness. My chest and right leg were covered with deep wounds. The dressings had to be changed regularly, and anesthesiologists would show up to dunk me under on those occasions too. Though my left hand was intact, it had been badly broken and was covered up, so I had zero hands in play. A bulky dressing covered my right eye, so I couldn't wear glasses, and I can't see much without them. I was running a fever nobody could explain. Your basic intensive-care-unit mattress is made, I would judge, of old tires filled with concrete. People kept insisting I had to eat (wounds can't heal unless you eat), but my appetite was far from robust. The sight, smell and thought of food made me sick. And physicians have the odd belief that people in intensive care units can't hear—or at any rate can't understand, having been rendered temporarily insane by the mattresses. I didn't learn much from the discussions that took place outside my grim cubicle that I didn't know already, but to hear yourself discussed as an abstract medical object is disconcerting and depressing.

One of my darkest memories is of one morning at roughly four in the intensive care unit under the harsh white-blue fluorescent light, a wall of instruments at my back, the concrete mattress underneath and a vague and harried nurse who had a certain Portland cement quality herself at the picture's edge: The joint otherwise empty—not many folks hang out in the ICU at four in the morning aside from the other badly sick inmates, one customer to a cubicle, as you can imagine a lively bunch. Stretched on a dissecting table (it felt like), hovering in a blue-white shaft of silence, pain and bright chrome flashes off weird instruments, sleepless except when I was drugged, disconnected from my boys, disconnected from grass, trees, piles of books, dawn, dusk and my own signature. I no longer had a signature. I had been right-handed and my right hand, what was left of it, was hidden under a million layers of surgical dressing, to emerge months later grotesquely transformed and no longer able to hold a pen. A lawyer had visited my cubicle so that I could transfer power of attorney to my wife. It was nice of him. Lawyers don't ordinarily make house calls. I'd had to sign the document and of course could not, but managed with a pen somehow connected to my bandaged, splinted left hand to make an X. To be reduced—the hotshot literary man, poet, author, deep reader—to signing myself with an X was an event that would have amused me under different circumstances.

With no signature, I worried about (what else?) how I would ever again buy things with credit cards—arguably a stupid thing to worry about in an intensive care unit. But credit cards represented for me, first and foremost, taking my wife out to dinner in Manhattan. She'd had the idea when we first met that, when I took her out, I was going to demand that she pay half. I had never encountered a girl with that misconception before, but my future wife moved in the highly cultured and (therefore) exquisitely egalitarian circles appropriate to a recent graduate of the nation's toniest architecture school. (Yale, of course.) That a lovely young woman should be *grateful* when her escort bought her dinner made me angry. I signed each charge slip with a flourish of disdain for the culture she had come from—a culture that was unworthy of her—and as a gesture of respect (every last signature) for my grandmother, who had always made it clear how much she approved of chivalrous gestures however small, fashionable or not. And of course it is always nice to come off as a big shot when you are merely not acting like a bum. So I loved signing charge slips in restaurants. We had been married eight years, but I still loved it. I hated to think I would never be able to do it again, therefore mourned of all ridiculous things my lost signature, when the mental effort would no doubt have been better directed at not dying.

The signature wasn't the worst of it. I hadn't seen my boys, who had just turned three and six, since the morning of the explosion. I had got the six-year-old a softball and his first baseball mitt for his birthday, and had been looking forward to the first time we would go out together and toss a ball around. What bothered me most in the hospital was that I would never be able to do that. It still bothers me acutely. But it is possible I gained more than I lost as a father. I never had the slightest doubt that fatherhood was my most important line of work, but nowadays each of their birthdays marks another year I have succeeded in being with them and doing what I can for them, and each year is an important victory. What I want most is to live long enough to see them safely into manhood—the common hope of all parents, I guess.

In time I invented a new game to replace baseball for me and my boys, now six and nine, called legitimate ball; the older player (the "dad") drop-kicks a kickball in a high, tight arc and calls it in the air: You get 900 points for catching a "legitimate" kick, a quarter million for snaring an off-course "quasi-legitimate" kick and 81 trillion if you catch an "illegitimate," which is ridiculously off course and usually lands on the roof. (As of this writing only one illegitimate kick has ever been caught, but it should actually have been called a "quasi" and is footnoted in the record book.) The goal of the game is to remember how many points you have. For nine-year-old players the goal is also to add up your score correctly. The scoring is complicated by the famous "free points" rule, which stipulates that the "dad" is allowed to hand out extra points to any player who needs cheering up; but when one fielder has been awarded a few million extra for cause (because he almost made a great catch, for example, or the ball bumped his nose), it often develops that the other fielder needs cheering up too. So the scores in legitimate ball can be substantial. Nevertheless it's a pretty good game and is near the point of catching on across the country—I hear more and more talk of Olympic demo-sport status. But I still miss baseball.

I hadn't yet departed the ICU when I told a sympathetic by-stander—my mother, I think—that I would be writing up this whole story as soon as I could manage it. A writer writes, for no particular reason; that's just the way it is. "If I couldn't write,"

James Thurber once said, "I couldn't breathe." I have felt that way myself since the day I learned to put letters on paper.

The moment he heard on the radio that I was hurt, a friend who lived several states away dropped what he was doing, got in his car and drove three hours to New Haven with no plan in mind but to do what he could. They wouldn't let him see me; he drove home. For years Nick Carriero and I had passed a postcard of Winston Churchill back and forth—whoever needed bucking up most at the moment got the picture. He brought it straight to my bedside.

Even in the depths of the ICU there were my brother to read me essays from E. B. White's *Second Tree from the Corner,* my parents to tell me how people all over the world were sending good wishes, a few close friends to keep me in touch (at least vaguely) with the normal working world I had exited with such a jolt, my wife first and foremost—I had a book to finish, and she began the process of reading me the manuscript and copying down the changes I dictated. Somehow the news even reached my cubicle that an older colleague, a rival of sorts, who had suspected (wrongly, it turns out) that he was smarter than me, had been so incensed to learn that his up-market literary agent was now mine too that he drove his car off the road, or something like that. It's all true: the writers you love, the work you need to do, the companionship of your family and closest friends, the one-upping of your professional colleagues—they ease a man's soul when he needs it most.

In trying to figure out today's strange nonjudgmental world, a good place to start is a 1936 Astaire-and-Rogers movie called *Follow the Fleet.* It has certain problems: Harriet Hilliard (of

Ozzie and Harriet in the 1950s and '60s) plays Ginger's un-glamorous sister with such dim mousiness that she is practically transparent, and even for a 1930s musical the plot is ridiculous. But Irving Berlin's music is wonderful and the dances rank among the century's significant artistic achievements. None of that matters for now; what matters is the headline of a con-cocted snippet of a news story that comes on screen when a plot turn needs explaining: FLEET IN CANAL ZONE—UNCLE SAM'S FIGHTING FORCES RETURN TO HOME WATERS AFTER WORLD CRUISE. Its tone is completely foreign and would be un-thinkable in a newspaper today. Why?

It's not just that we no longer refer to the United States as "Uncle Sam," it's that the headline has a firsthand tone and sounds like neighborhood gossip (*Aunt Sally's cocker spaniels. Uncle Sam's fighting forces. Mr. Feinstein's wretched stamp collection*). The imaginary headline-writer was not reporting a fact, as today's reporters strive to, with the outside-observer neutral-ity of a scientist recording in his lab notebook the dalliances of cockroaches; he was writing *from the inside,* as an American de-scribing America.

American culture was shaped in this period by a literary de-vice: Americans thought of America as a person. That liter-ary device was a dressmaker's dummy, imparting shape to the finished product though it was hidden beneath the fabric. America was a person with a particular personality, habits and viewpoint.

Call him Fred or, if you prefer, Andy or George, three choices in all; the American Person as a literary device was hugely im-portant, because it put each American (however cranky or puny or unworthy, cynical, crotchety, atypical) in contact with the nation. The Canonical American conspicuously failed to reflect certain parts of America, particularly black parts. Yet every last person in the country was invited to step into this rent-a-tuxedo, this evening-gown-for-hire; you could put it on at whim. Norman Podhoretz describes his experiences as a young Jew of the early 1950s in the formerly gentile world of Columbia University, taking a literary classics course in which the works of Jewish writers were not in evidence; "far from being excluded, I was being invited *in*."

Representation or symbolism is a complex proposition. One thing *standing for* something else, yet not *being* that other thing or even very like it: Westminster Abbey symbolizes and embodies the English people, not one of whom is a pile of rock. George Washington embodied America although he was richer than most of his countrymen and had worse teeth. Symbolism starts in dreams, and so does literature. Literature rests on dreaming the way Christianity is built on the Bible. In modern times we pull further and further away from literature and symbolism; become ever more literal-minded. In his heyday the Canonical American was universally imagined to be a white male, to the extent people imagined him in any particular way at all. But he is untenable today not on account of his white maleness but because of the premise. He had to be *somebody* and therefore could not exactly match *everybody*. In the more sophisticated America of the past, you could feel yourself (whoever you were) to be symbolized by a white (usually Anglo-Saxon Protestant) male the way you could tolerate a violin concerto being performed by a musician who wasn't your ethnic or genetic type, if he was true to the score.

When I say that the Canonical American has become untenable, I mean we could not revive him even if we wanted to. But that's not why he vanished to begin with; he disappeared because he was killed. I'll show you how. The whole process rests on a social transformation so pervasive it is the air we breathe; hundreds of books have discussed the deep changes of the late 1960s, but few have pointed out how they hinge, finally, on the intelligentsia's having taken over the elite.

———

One of the Canonical American's most important contributions was to make it possible for the nation to be judgmental. Yes, it's true; once upon a time, we were a downright judgmental bunch.

A 1937 *Life* magazine. News item: New York police foil a robbery. They'd noticed the criminals lurking and guessed what was coming. "The picture at right," reads a caption, "shows the two dead bandits lying in the street where police dropped them." "Neatest trap of the year," says *Life*. That tone is called gloating. Two dead bandits, neat trap, *good news*. For violent criminals this long-ago society bristled with contempt. It did not tolerate violent criminals. It was judgmental.

Terrorism "has become a part of life," according to a political scientist quoted in the *Wall Street Journal*. "We're no longer quite so surprised" when the bombs go off. Americans, says the headline approvingly, are growing MORE RESILIENT. *(But let's not be too judgmental. There's not a judgmental word in this book. We need to be open-hearted, loving and nonjudgmental. An older sister figure to whom they can talk about problems, knowing she won't be shocked or judgmental.)* "Experts say [*Wall Street Journal*, summer '96] that this life-goes-on attitude clearly is becoming more prevalent within the American psyche." (Experts at what, reading the newspaper? Just so long as they're experts.) "Across the nation, bombings are soaring [*The New York Times*, summer '96]. They increased by more than 50 percent in the last five years, and have nearly tripled over the last decade."

Don't be surprised, don't be upset, don't be judgmental. *Be passive:* morally, spiritually. Our "resilience," our "practicality" (another word from the *Journal*), our unsurprise, our noble disdain for "being judgmental"—how could it all *possibly* be just the effect of violence and no part of the cause?

And didn't we used to be, in the United States of America, the least passive country in the world? How did this happen to us?

———

Nowadays we get the newspapers delivered, and weekday mornings a few minutes after seven I head up our long driveway to the mailbox, usually with my younger boy. A mid-October day: the yellow leaves sift down in the breeze, acorns plop straight to the driveway as if their parachutes hadn't opened. They create an air of comic surprise—so long as you don't get hit by one. We're in the bowl of a streambed and the valley collects mist on fall mornings, graying the brown trunks of the oak, tulip trees and maple. Tumbled heaps of white mums and magenta asters are drunk and disorderly at this time of year, falling over. But they have the appeal of Marilyn Monroe with her hair in disarray. The whole garden does—brown leaves tangled everywhere and the shadow of death. We are in a region of the year where the summer birds are mostly gone and the winter ones haven't arrived yet, and when there is no breeze there is perfect silence on our walks up the driveway—aside from my six-year-old singing "Puttin' on the Ritz," of course, with tap barrages to go along. Both my boys study tap dancing and are good at it, vastly better than I could ever have been, and the six-year-old can't stop dancing. There was unhappiness at the start of this year's tap class because a third boy had joined, and my boys regard it as their God-given right to have all the girls in the class strictly to themselves. They would not be opposed to writing such a stipulation into law. If I ever catch them mounting a petition drive for a citizens' initiative referendum I will know what to expect. Luckily the third boy quit quickly, and things are back to normal.

Thank God the leaves turn and acorns plop and my boy walks beside me to get the paper in the morning, and a man doesn't need to think about bombs, crime and society full-time. For I have to confess that the only society I care deeply about in the end is my family and a few friends, and I am not sure whether each man cultivating his garden is not our only shot at saving the world.

CHAPTER THREE

THE FIRST TIME I got wheeled out of the intensive care unit to a standard hospital room it didn't work, and I got wheeled right back. I encountered during this first foray a fantastically sweet nurse and a lot of commotion—my memories of the episode are discontinuous; but it turned out that my condition was unstable and I got sent back to the ICU. A few days later, when I was finally capable of getting by without constant monitoring, I was moved to an ordinary room in the plastic surgery area.

There I encountered an even sweeter nurse, named Rhonda Laidlaw. She was chief nurse on my case, and it is hard to convey how much less awful it is to face total incapacity with a good and noble nurse taking care of you. Some of the doctors who worked on me were brilliant, and a couple were wonderful, but the few times I encountered nobility among medical people it was in the form of a nurse. Rhonda was the noblest of all. Fate owed me one, and so I got Rhonda.

Soon after emerging from the ICU I had my first talk with the FBI. (Agents may have visited me in the ICU also, but I don't remember.) Ron and Ken, of whom I saw a lot over the next several years—Ron smiling to compensate for Ken's usually looking worried. I liked them both; in a cant-ridden age I admired their cant-freedom, and it was clear also that they each had a personal interest in catching criminals and would love to catch this one. The grim chuckling in Ron's eyes that the PR man in his brain is always shushing (in the interest of a professional demeanor to match his neat tie and shiny shoes) is reassuring because it is genuine. His smile is interrupted only by an occasional quick wince that is so deep it throws off shock waves that make you wince too. The wince accompanies his restrained account of some unbelievably idiotic idea (of course he will never put it in those terms) that other law enforcement people have cooked up, or a promising lead that led nowhere.

Lawmen, medical personnel and reporters are three groups with whom I was destined to spend more time than I ever had before. My respect for the first two shot up. I will say more about reporters later. A few are an honor to know. Between lawmen and reporters on the whole it is impossible, however, not to notice this difference: Most lawmen seem to hate criminals, and most reporters couldn't care less.

Maybe I am wrong. I conducted no scientific surveys, and such evidence as I have I could be misinterpreting. What I do know is that the reporters who crossed my path mostly wanted to discharge their crime-related moral duties by lavishing smarmy pity on the victim, like a maiden aunt deploying damp kisses. Reporters have developed a remarkable gift for making you feel dirty.

The FBI men wanted to know everything: everywhere I had

visited; especially every place I had lectured. I repeatedly found myself describing people who must have sounded strange but couldn't possibly, I kept saying, have mailed a bomb. I was sure I had never encountered such a person. The lists went on and on, usually until a medical staffer wandered by to do some procedure or other.

From the day I was hurt to the day the likely culprit was arrested roughly three years later (he was a mathematician, it turned out, living alone in a rustic cabin near Lincoln, Montana) the manhunt rarely left our minds. Events as the months passed made the tension tighten, not slack off.

He hasn't struck in the same place twice, Ron told us at the start, *yet.* In truth no one had a clue what the man had in mind. When Professor Charles Epstein and I were injured in June 1993, it was Mr. Bucolic-Cottage-in-the-Countryside's first outing in several years. (Epstein is a distinguished geneticist at the University of California's San Francisco Medical School. It is an honor to have been his cotarget.) When he struck next, in late '94, he killed a man—an advertising executive and philanthropist with a family and children and, the evidence suggests, a big heart. An especially good man represents to a wicked one the ultimate danger—the conscience and justice he hates and can never silence. ("Conscience is a Jewish invention," Hitler said; it wouldn't surprise me if the bomber felt the same. Or maybe he believes that the military-industrial complex invented it, some slow afternoon.) So here we are a year and a half after I was hurt—no arrest in sight, the criminal whetting his knife and the FBI with no idea what is coming next.

The next move turns out to be mine, accidentally. The FBI is unenthusiastic about my talking publicly about the crime.

Helping the investigation is always my main goal. But when the distinguished technology journalist Steven Levy interviews me in late summer of '94, I can't help mentioning that I regard the bomber as evil and a coward and don't give a damn about his opinions on any topic. The interview is finally published in late spring '95 in the *New York Times Magazine*. The bomber is thought to read the *Times*, and has sent it various communiqués over the years. An FBI man tells me, "Maybe this will flush him out."

By this time I am able to drive again, and many evenings when I leave work and climb into my elderly Honda for the homeward trip, I hesitate before reaching round the wheel with my left hand, as I do, to turn the key; I leave the door ajar to allow for rapid egress should a bomb explode. Though I doubt the open door would have helped much. Sometimes I'd think, the instant before turning the key, This is it; my highly nuanced bomb sense tells me it's gonna blow. I would even climb out, sometimes, for a quick and utterly pointless inspection. Turns out my highly nuanced bomb sense is no good.

In summer '95, not long after the Levy interview appeared, Hut Man favors me with a personal note. Chris Hatchell and I glance at it together; we confer for ten seconds and Chris is off immediately to the local FBI office. Toward midnight Agent Ron phones: The FBI crime lab has established that the letter is genuine. And this same day, Ron tells us, the bomber has killed another man in California.

I am the only target ever to rate après-bomb fan mail from Saint John of Montana. To what do I owe the honor? The instant I glanced at the letter, I thought I knew; the answer leaped out. He referred to the epilogue of my 1991 book *Mirror Worlds*. Evidently he has some sort of grudge against technology. (He used a typewriter and rode a bus—go figure; but the machines he loved best are the ones that kill people.) He picked me out originally, my guess is, with no idea who I was aside from some guy who worked with computers. He discovered later from the *Mirror Worlds* epilogue that he had succeeded in locating one of the very few persons in the field who doesn't *like* computers. Yes they are great in principle, still promising in practice and have revolutionized science and engineering, but I worry about their tendency to bring out the worst in us. I discuss these worries in the *Mirror Worlds* epilogue.

A man hates above all to look like a fool. To be loathed is one thing; to imagine people laughing at you is another, for many people far worse. When he saw *Mirror Worlds,* my hunch is, the bomber pictured the world laughing at him, which made him furious. *Mirror Worlds* was (Lord knows) no bestseller but did get a fair amount of attention, and came out in paperback and in German and Japanese too. With the exaggerated self-regard of the hardened criminal, not to mention the mathematician— and our culprit is also, it so happens, a former Berkeley professor and, almost *too* perfect, *a Harvard grad!*—he no doubt saw himself as the main topic of conversation and (consequently) ridicule in every *Bierstube* and Sushi bar from Bremerhaven to Yatsuhiro. (*"Was für ein echt Schwein-faced Dummkopf, eh, Horst?"* [Laughter]) Not to mention every living room of Middle America. ("I jes' finished *Mirror Worlds* and lan' sakes, Mabel, that there genius bombed the only computer scientist in the whole dang country who hates computers! Don't that jes' have Harvard written all over it!" [Laughter]) My guess is that the bomber wrote me in a spiteful rage. In any case the letter arrived, and another man was dead, and the tension ratcheted higher.

The Bomber's Prayer: "May the Lord strike you dead, or better yet may I strike you dead and the Lord merely grant me the necessary skill with explosives."

And so I would leave my car door ajar and frown intently as I started the engine.

In the hospital I didn't worry about my own safety but did, all the time, about my family's at home. We didn't know where the bomber lived or what he planned. For all we knew, he lived in New Haven. During the first few weeks and at tense points thereafter, we had policemen around our home. My sensitive and too-imaginative older boy pointed out what he saw as the obvious problems: They were guarding the front door, but what about the sliding doors leading out to the deck in back? Our lot has a large perimeter, and the defensive line was full of holes. And how far can you reassure a worried child that he is safe and all is well when his father has just been blown up by a bomb? He needed his parents; we were unspeakably lucky to have his uncles and aunts and grandparents and our good friends to step in, but when a six-year-old's mother is gone all day, his father all night too, and the grounds swarm with police—how far can you reassure him? The bomb that hurt Professor Epstein was addressed to his home, and he opened the package in his kitchen. If his teenage daughter had been in the room, she would have been hurt, maybe killed. So we had to worry; we had no choice, because we knew our criminal to be a man who would not scruple to murder children.

In the hospital my health was no pretty picture: my shattered right hand, broken left hand, the lines of surgical staples holding my chest closed, the regions on my legs where layers of skin had been sliced off to provide raw material for chest grafts. Lying flat on your back all day makes you weak—when I reached the point where I could sit in a chair for a few minutes, it turned out to be hard work; the first time I tried it, I fainted. To counteract possible blood clotting when you are bedridden, they inject you three times a day with a nasty substance that burns, and eventually you are covered with bruises from the damned injections, and it takes a good long time to figure out where the next one should go. Various other grotesque health issues. Lots more heavy surgery to look forward to.

There were long-term questions also about how my health would turn out: to what extent I would have a right hand, to what extent a right eye, how much pain as a regular thing; how far I would be able to slip back into a normal routine. Some people (one surgeon thoughtfully pointed out to my wife) never did come back from a blow like this. They sat at home and collected disability checks for the rest of their lives.

A man's health is a monumentally boring topic, and I yield to no one in degree of boredom with my own. This was so in the hospital too, although there boredom takes on a grim edge. My chief surgeon was attempting to save a piece of my hand by reupholstering the blown-up right edge with skin from somewhere else. The triumphal first week's surgery had made the attempt possible. He had been able to locate more bits and pieces of my wrist than he had anticipated, and had pieced them together into a thing that sort of looked like a wrist in the sense that a plastic car model assembled by a very young child sort of looks like a car. Maybe half the pieces got left out, and maybe the finished product is encased in model cement like a large plastic bug in amber, but a kid has to start somewhere. I don't intend that as a criticism—the operation was (as I say) a surgical tour de force. In any case, my arm was stitched to my side for almost a month like a teacup handle. You can imagine how much fun that was—or if you can't, so much the better. It wasn't clear whether the maneuver would work, and many bedside medical conferences took place. My wife was in on all of them. As for me, I wanted to hear the sheer minimum. I just don't have the stomach for it. The procedure came off as planned; the question then became whether I would be able to do anything with the piece of right hand I had got. But when it finally came out from under wraps months later, it was months more before I could even bring myself to look at it. I have never been one for freak shows and I am "sensitive" (to dress up an ugly condition in a nice word) to the point of physical illness.

Traveling all over creation flat on my back with no more control over my progress or destination than a log in a river— that was my defining hospital experience. The Yale medical complex is a village of buildings all connected by bridges. So my right eardrum, for example, had a hole blown in it just for good measure, and the ear clinic was about twelve miles from my room, and you rolled through a hundred random buildings along the way. I had to make that trip on several occasions, and each time it felt like driving the length of New Jersey. You roll down endless hallways—where the sun comes through the big sealed windows and echoes in a cackling evil glare off shiny floors and the glass-fronted frames of hospital art on the walls (the lovely-sunset photos, the picturesque-boats-at-harbor photos, as if when you are sick and only allowed to eat mush you ought to be forced to look at mush also)—and you never step outside; even ten seconds would have done good; you roll instead on a stretcher covered by a couple of sheets. People slice into your field of view at odd angles as if you are peering at Manhattan skyscrapers from a convertible; their heads floating far above—you cannot, at these strange angles, read their eyes; but you don't want to anyway, and they fall back as the stretcher rolls on, and picturesque fishing boats at anchor glide from your feet up past your head and are gone. In this state it is just barely possible to feel like a man at all. Once again I lost my sense of humor completely. But your sense of humor and sense of dignity are basically the same thing. Humor is the basis of dignity, and when it goes you are lost. At times I almost wished I could close my eyes and turn into that log riding briskly and oblivious through the fresh air. Only my wife walking beside me held things together. The fundamental things apply. And there was worse than that in the form of a videotape shot by a well-meaning friend, of my boys spending an afternoon at a local pool; the nurses were constantly threatening to roll in a VCR and play it for me. But seeing my boys romping with some other child's parents when I should have been with them, seeing how they got on in the world without a father—it was more than I could take.

Yet hospital life had its lighter moments. My wife would show up early in the morning and leave around dinnertime; my parents would often come and read to me in the evenings—with no hands there was nothing whatever I could do. My wife learned how to do everything immediately. Before long she was patiently teaching things to the staff. Now and then I'd get wheeled off and slung on some sort of mammoth cranelike device into a whirlpool bath. I never got a good look at it, but pictured a towering construction crane with hefty stabilizer legs and a chugging million-horsepower diesel motor. (Is that right?) Before I'd depart they would shoot me up with a special painkiller that dopifies a person in a curious and not altogether unpleasant way. The side effects include poetry recitation, starting with *The Iliad* in Greek, to the confusion of the clinical staff. I don't know much of *The Iliad* in Greek, but what I did know came in handy owing to this particular side effect. I do know a lot of poetry in English, more than I had imagined, and under the game rules for this drug, an injectee when he is done with Greek may switch to another language of his choice. No doubt it took a lot of tinkering for the pharmacologists to make it all come out just right. At any rate the old, discredited assumptions, large and small, proved repeatedly to be correct: Great poetry is a consolation. Learning great words by heart is a good idea.

Much as I hated the hospital and longed to get out of it, I was unclear and downhearted about the future. I didn't know how to picture life without a right hand or normal right eye. I had got quite a lot of use out of my right hand. You'll learn to write with your left, people told me, but I only half believed them. No one told me I would learn to paint with my left, and I wouldn't have believed them if they had.

My brother brought me a boom box and at night I would listen to music on CDs. In the hospital my sleep was heavily drugged and opaque. I rarely remembered any dreams. When I did they were grotesque and often involved my boys, which made it worse. But ordinarily my sleep was steel black. When I got out of the hospital and pushed away (like a boat making for home in heavy weather) from the opaque black of powerful sedatives, and the black turned gradually translucent and I could make out dreams again, it was a sort of emotional crisis. These dreams were full up (naturally) with exactly the thoughts I deliberately suppressed during the day. (The "secret" of dreams is a thing that, I believe, almost all dream researchers and dream philosophers know, yet they rarely say it clearly. The basic fact about sleep is that your guard is down. You are badly fixed to ward off stray golf balls or unwanted thoughts. And so at night, the thoughts you have suppressed during the day emerge. Naturally Freud believed that a dream was necessarily the expression of a wish; in Freudian Vienna one often suppressed one's wishes.) I dreamed repeatedly about the things I used to do and never would again—playing tennis, which I enjoyed but which never mattered to me much; swimming at the beach, which mattered more; playing the piano, still more. Sometimes my dreams got ingenious—a long, strange story I still recall about a trombone player, which I recognized afterward as a rumination on the topic of instruments a person might play with only one good hand. Every once in a while the action would come to a halt in a blast of light that woke me up and was unmistakable.

When my life came to a screeching halt and I woke up in the hospital, I was the driver who only remembers at the instant he slams on the brakes that he has piled a ton of baggage on the rear seat, and it is all streaking toward the back of his head. The hardest question I faced in the hospital was how to reconstruct my life. It was a stickier proposition than you might expect.

A recurring event with a distinctive flavor gives you the sensation of life looping back on itself. It is an odd sensation, but valuable. Your goal in life is to defeat each moment's propensity to be over before you know what is happening. That is why the best prose is the grittiest: you score vicarious experience points as you read. The greatest English prose passage of all, the first fifty pages of Joyce's *Ulysses,* is simultaneously the most musical and most concrete. Joyce wrote about fried eggs the way Velázquez painted them, as if the whole of art came down to the true and actual fried-eggness of fried eggs. And it does. The value of art is not ideas but fried eggs.

Listening to Palestrina's *Missa Brevis,* a mass for unaccompanied four-voice choir published in 1570, is for me a flavorful, recurring event that makes time loop back in an oxbow. Describing music is a waste, but the *Missa Brevis* is simple and sublime and rustles with the poignant colored shadows that minor triads cast on major keys. It glides past like the tall triangle of a sailboat in a dream, carrying people you would love to talk to but no longer can. Describing music is a waste.

This mass sailed into my life on my twentieth birthday, when my best friend gave me a recording. On the eve of that birthday I stayed up most of the night writing poems in an apotheosis of undergraduateness. I published a few of the night's products, suitably buffed up, in a literary quarterly—my first publication, aside from student newspaper stuff. My work at that period had the occasional decent line but overall must have been as appealing as a squashed squirrel by the roadside. But eventually my poetry got better. I have always been a devoted and solitary poet, moved only rarely to publish. People still write poetry today, but no one reads it, a freakish anomaly of supply and demand—as if society had forgotten to notify a certain whalebone-corset plant or detachable-wing-collar factory that tastes have changed. So the product builds up, neatly packaged, and in the end the producers are surrounded and cut off. Unfortunately a poet writes because he can't help it, not because it serves any purpose, and poem-writing today has the futility of alchemy.

I loved the Palestrina mass the first time I heard it, love it still, listened to it in the hospital—and it was the last piece of music I ever played on the piano. I was a bad pianist but liked to play and miss it. In the spring of 1993 I bought the *Missa Brevis* score and read through the Kyrie and Credo a few times haltingly. But it is comforting, in the end, that the *Missa Brevis* is the last thing I ever played, because it is not piano music. It is vocal music, and I can still sing.

I had the habit, as I suspect many bad pianists and probably some good ones do, of listening to recorded piano music under the conceit that I was playing it. More than a year passed between the day I was hurt and the day I was finally able to listen once more to solo piano music, which used to be what I mainly listened to. The piano had been useful to me not only for entertainment but in writing down music I had composed—though reliance on the piano when you are composing is a bad habit. I have kicked it, more or less.

Painting and writing are the areas in which I feel like a professional, and I earn my living as a technologist. That I write music also will come off as an odd assertion, like a NASCAR race driver mentioning casually to his pit crew that he is a Yiddish dramatist on the side—sure you are, Bubba, they tell him soothingly, just get back in the car. But the contention is not as odd as it looks. Nothing in art is foreign to me, but I'm no good at anything else, and there is nothing abnormal about my interests except the way they are distributed. Melodies come naturally to me, although in music (as opposed to painting) my style is retrograde, old-fashioned but lyrical.

———

I am rotten at everything that is not art; have succeeded in computer science only by forcing software into a strictly aesthetic mold, making it a design issue like architecture or painting. I hate machines except insofar as they are beautiful (as the best are). I am not so much bad at organizational and administrative tasks as stupefyingly awful, with a desk and entire office that curdles the blood of those who are merely messy as hell. Any space in which I work turns immediately to chaos. I am a barely decent teacher at best; I try hard but am invariably too fast or too slow, because I am a failure, also, at dealing with people except one at a time. You would do better from the standpoint of scintillating conversation to invite a bucket of plankton to a party than invite me. And I would as soon attend your party as I would a public pigeon pummeling. I am bad at money, can't manage to save my receipts for income tax purposes even when my wife has reduced the problem to first-grade terms ("here is a big box; put them here"), and as a result pay a larger percentage of my income in taxes than any other person in history and am in line for the first Taxpayer Recognition Medal ever to be awarded by the IRS's Sucker Appreciation Division. I don't cook, don't ski, don't fish, don't skate, don't hike, make ordinary household repairs grudgingly after putting them off for a minimum of six years in hopes the afflicted object will be struck by a meteorite and demolished, forget to look at my calendar and skip appointments, forget to write the appointments in my calendar in the first place, forget where my calendar is, forget if I even *have* a calendar. But nothing in art is foreign to me.

And that accounts for a good deal of my perplexity and bitterness in the hospital and afterward. I went into computer science at a time when I wanted a trade, a way to make a living doing something of practical, nut-and-bolts value. Only a few people have ever grasped what a bizarre choice I made in becoming (of all things) a software researcher. But you don't become a tinsmith, either, because you have any special liking or genius for it; you go into tinsmithing because you are able to do the work, the opportunity presents itself and it is an honest way to earn a living. However strange the choice—and technology research is, granted, not a *lot* like tinsmithing under any circumstances—it still strikes me as reasonable or at any rate inevitable. But I had outgrown this arrangement. The romantic idea of spending your days in the real world and your nights writing or painting is by no means untenable and even has certain advantages, but it gets old. It had suddenly become clear that I could easily die without having accomplished more than the tiniest fraction of what I had wanted and expected to accomplish.

With my right hand gone I believed I would never paint again. The mental stockpile of pictures I had worked on assiduously over the years, with only an occasional quick sketch to record a detail (although I never forgot any detail of a mental painting)—none of those pictures, I supposed, would ever be painted. And at my pilot's controls the ground loomed up suddenly, the canned warning message thoughtfully built in by the manufacturer for just such an occasion triggered—"wrong career, wrong career"—and gales of mocking laughter and moments later the smash, and I could picture all too clearly what

n the form of
ddenness and
lder boy, also,
lf away from
cked.

l: "D. H. Gelernter,
nto a decorative rose

June and all of July,

rm, the brook behind
sound of its rushing,
Brisk and sunny with
treet overflowing with
utumn trees. You smell
l tramping moss, slick
ersweet berries trailing
e ground. Back in our
e to the brook down
best living arrangement
art-time on a New En-
uttered, attended to his
engagement on princi-
tion. But the position I
crowded suburb with a
dly old-fashioned place
s to warn each other of

f the pond at dusk I am
arily toward the rushing
nger boy proposes to go
ts everything in perspec-
ky life: The problems are
ntirely; it is an imperfect

thing, but the amazing luck stands next to you
your small boy, who adds his bit to the all-over
then dances his way home beside you—and the
who stayed home because he couldn't tear him
his 1932 Hardy Boys mystery: *While the Clock*

CHAPTER FOUR

So I come home, and my right hand is bandaged and splinted and has metal rods sticking out like toothpicks in a baked potato. The rods are holding my wrist together; they are supposed to come out in another operation later on. I had worn an eye patch in the hospital. I no longer need it for protection, the damaged eye is stable, but I don't take it off right away. I dread the half-blurred view when the eye is uncovered. But the elastic of the patch gives you a headache eventually—probably that's why pirates are always in such a bad mood—and I don't relish looking any stranger than strictly necessary, so hesitantly I remove it. And the world goes blurry and I walk around in a fog.

I struggle to get through the night. It's hard to drift off, my dreams are bad news and the dark birds of pain gather as I sleep. They shadow me like vultures all day and settle in at night, grabbing hold of the branches. It takes time to shake them off in the morning. Awakening I swallow painkillers and, until they kick in, sit at the edge of the mattress not moving, unable to. I am the picture of sloth—sitting around all day, moving slowly and uncertainly when I am forced to. But am also suffering from the emotional equivalent of an out-of-control pulse.

I don't know how to confront the world one-handed and one-eyed. In the hospital I didn't need to confront it, but now I do, and there are precious few activities that don't involve clear vision and your right hand. My deep confusion is not a question of everyday tactics, it is the the rest of my life: Permanent damage brings the whole rest of your life into play, pulls everything out of every closet and drawer and dumps it in a pile in front of you, and wherever you go, there is the rest-of-your-life problem to climb over. How will you do it in this suddenly modified body, with this suddenly unclear view?

The phone rings and my wife picks up. It's a friend of mine, but I stand three feet away rigidly still as she repeats the message and hangs up. I am incapable of taking the phone. Something's baking in the oven and the timer goes off, but grabbing it out is a two-handed operation and I can't visualize the steps you would need if you were to do it one-handed, so I stand (it feels like) on the cliff's edge looking at the surf a hundred feet below. It is not easy to convey the sense of stupefying unfamiliarity. As a graduate student I made a brief visit to Paris. I hadn't been in France since childhood, and the strangeness of every texture transfixed me. One time I milled around outside a bakery for half an hour plotting the purchase of a croissant, contemplating the French I would speak (six words), the likely response—and basking in the dazzling strangeness, pacing a hundred-foot stretch of sidewalk in slow motion. The pavement zigging in and zagging out to accommodate the uneven fronts of old buildings, the gutter down the sidewalk's center, the Euro-cars I had read about but never seen before, the singsong beep of an ambulance, the beautiful dark-haired girl wearing plastic bracelets and smelling like laundry detergent who glances at me as we pass (and spends the rest of her life wondering, we can safely assume, "That mysterious stranger—who could he possibly have been?"). Even when I am alone in my hotel room I hesitate to touch things and spend long motionless periods admiring them. Pathological sensitivity is a disease from which I have always suffered; it has certain rewards, but not many. Paris was fascinating whereas my house after I had been hurt is alarming and oppressive, but the enveloping uncertainty is the same.

My confusion is not merely abstract. I can no longer cut food with a knife or tie shoelaces. It is hard to wash your hands when you are down to only one. I still have these problems today and always will, and they amount to zero—but they took getting used to. I pull a heavy book off the shelf with my left hand, which is not used to heavy books, and it falls spreadeagle to the floor. Because it is hard to manage a belt and I'm sore all over from wounds and graft sites, I go around in sweatpants and baggy shirts—the mental patient look. I think often of the clothes I was wearing when the bomb blew: a new beige sport-jacket and new loafers, old pants, newish watch—they are gone. I envy my old self for the way I bought and wore clothes like a normal person.

The hospital staff had been first-rate, by and large, but did not distinguish itself in the matter of my wedding ring. A nurse had emerged from the operating room complex during my first surgery and handed the thing in a plastic bag to my sister-in-law. It was covered with blood and gore. (Among our many allies, my brother and his wife were closest and most essential. That they lived nearby was another dazzling piece of good luck.) My wife set store by that wedding ring. She'd had a theory that you were supposed to wear it full time, even asleep—naturally I assumed she was kidding, but when it became clear she wasn't, I manfully gave it a try. (In actual practice there is no such thing as a male who can sleep with a ring on, as any anthropologist will tell you.) My sister-in-law cleaned it and we got the ring back, but it turns out that you need two hands to manage a ring.

There used to be a routine in the evening. I would tell one boy a story while my wife read to the other, and then we would switch; but I don't have the energy to do that any more, or do anything else, and the children are sympathetic but don't know what to think.

Outdoors is worst. I venture outside on a warm August day. My arm cradled in a sling with rods sticking out is no inducement to strolling, and the blurred eye separates me from the world. I feel acutely the slick bottoms of my loafers, as if I am about to go sliding down this slight slope of lawn. Because I have no depth vision, every tree branch is poised to smack me in the face. Damage to my right cornea makes the sun's glare oppressive. I retreat inside, scuttle for shelter. Shortly before I was hurt I had assembled a child-sized basketball hoop for my boys. I look at it on my way in and imagine that it is the last thing I will ever build for them. Even when I am inside, it's odd: The outdoors doesn't exist. I look out the window and nothing registers, as if I were looking at a gray scrim.

It is disorienting to be home during working hours. When I am not out seeing some doctor or other I am usually on a livingroom sofa feeling as if I am on the floor of a cave. It is a biggish room with a high ceiling and windows concentrated along a narrow eastern wall—not a bad room, but somber in the daytime. There's a piano in one corner, and the walls are covered with crammed bookcases and my old paintings—some are college era, others dashed off during the years that ended with the bomb, the years when I spent too much time on the wrong things. Each in its own way is painful to look at and reminds me of the paintings now trapped in my head forever. The house is too quiet. If the boys are home they are usually in some other room, because it is important that no one crash into me. So I sit silently in my sweatpants and baggy shirt, nearly vibrating in pained confusion.

I need cool: wet washcloth for the fevered forehead. Cool will consist, for me, of intellectual stimulation that has no emotional content—zero. That kind of stimulation will be (when I find it) profoundly soothing, unspeakably. It will take me a little while to locate the mother lode of cool, but when I do, life will change.

———

Despite anguished confusion I am getting a little work done— I finish tidying up my nearly completed book and then dictate to my wife, in rough bursts like a lawnmower that won't quite start, a paper about Moses for the journal *Conservative Judaism*. The editor is Rabbi Benjamin Scolnic, a remarkable scholar who is co-authoring a new Bible commentary that will be used (I expect) in synagogues all over the world; he is a pulpit rabbi too, at a synagogue not far from New Haven. He visited me in the hospital and at home—I had heard about but never met him. The first time he came by, he asked how I was doing, and then mentioned casually that "when they catch this guy I would string him up on the Green." Then we talked about Biblical literature. Sometimes he has an angelic, gently amused expression that would make a rock like him, other times a dead-pan half-asleep look that complements his superb comic timing and makes it clear that, if he hadn't been otherwise booked, he could have been a superb standup comedian. He has great learning and an incomprehensible love of sports. If he were a Chassidic *rebbe* there would be tales about him.

He wasn't entirely serious in proposing a public hanging, but wasn't quite kidding either. The comment put him in a different moral world from the sleazeball reporters who plagued me. A man wants to act, not be acted upon. Self-pity is a pile of bricks on your chest, and your real friends help you heave it off. Those of us who hate today's victim culture don't hate it because we are Teddy Roosevelts aiming to build character and toughen people up (not that there is anything wrong with that program); we hate it because it inflicts harm. When you encourage a man to see himself as a victim of *anything*—crime, poverty, bigotry, bad luck—you are piling bricks on his chest. How we can logically justify as a nation being in favor of self-pity and against smoking is not clear, but the inconsistency may be yet another symptom of our blindness to all things spiritual. Our fanatic drive to crush and eradicate every threat to our physical well-being has a sad air of compulsive busywork about it—we are the Lady Macbeth society, obsessively washing our hands to cleanse ourselves of sin, perfecting and *purifying* our bodies (no barest trace of "chemicals" allowed!), as if that will cure our sick souls.

(If you browse the New Age section of your local bookstore—spiritual healing, power of myth, Bill Moyers—you will discover an amazing accomplishment. Never mind the schools, universities, public affairs; in our missionary zeal we have even succeeded in taking religion out of religion.)

A visitor who says "let's go get those bastards and string 'em up" is (on the other hand) inviting you to put your injury to use, to do something *to make the world better,* because when you string up a murderer you do make the world better, don't you? That's one less murderer. I am not yet addressing the question of capital punishment and Rabbi Scolnic wasn't either. Murderers can be removed from circulation in other ways. I am only explaining why this person made such perfect sense to me and was so welcome. He reminded me of my grandfather, who is a rabbi also.

So I am working to the extent I can manage. But am deeply confused about the future and everything else. Don't know whether I still have a chance to do the work I am supposed to do, or have blown it forever. Mainly I sit around in pain and silence.

———

When I got home from the hospital my wife gave me a ten-page list of names: reporters, TV producers, editors and whatnot who had phoned with interview requests. They all wanted me to call back. Some had left detailed messages.

I started the game in a pro-press frame of mind. In my old life I had talked to a fair number of technology reporters, and found them smart and conscientious on the whole. And a writer, like it or not, depends on publicity. In any case, when a man gets blown up by a mail bomb there is a news story in there someplace. There was nothing wrong with reporters wanting to interview me; I planned to talk to them, within reason, and have in fact talked to many. When the suspect was captured years later and I published a piece in *Time,* a local newspaper ran a headline claiming "Gelernter Finally Speaks." Wrong; I had already spoken at length. But my experience with the press overall was so eye-opening, it forced me to rethink everything I knew about American society.

My first week out of the hospital felt as if I had ambled up to a crowd of reporters, greeted them amiably and they had all jumped me—a cartoon football pileup with me at the bottom. When you get hit by a journalistic feeding frenzy you are stunned at first; then you pull away in disgust and dark amusement.

I hadn't anticipated becoming a celebrity, and our number is in the book. I arrive home and sit down, and the phone starts to ring. People want to interview me for newspapers or magazines, or put me on radio or TV. Print reporters make the calls themselves. TV interviewers are too important for that, so they make their producers do it. (The producers who call are nearly all female—possibly it is a female occupation nowadays, or possibly women are easier to bully, or more likely to succeed, or less likely to suffer disabling phone phobias. Surveys reveal that 54 percent of American males would sooner kiss a gorilla than phone somebody they don't know.)

Typically there are calm periods and heavy ones, each several hours long. During calm periods we get a couple of calls; during heavies, the phone rings every ten minutes or worse. The timing of the periods is unpredictable, but for a couple of weeks there are several heavies per day. The storm kicks up again whenever there is a new development in the case or a rumor of one. Soon after I get home we acquire a fax machine to help keep me in touch with the office; during frenzy weeks, we can count on a couple of faxes a day also. Reporters bang on the door infrequently, but now and then we see TV crews prowling the street out front in station wagons like sharks eyeing a shark cage. One especially revolting local station runs pictures of our youngest boy romping out front with a babysitter. Later on when I am back at work, reporters feel free during frenzy weeks to wander around the halls bothering people until someone calls the police. I remember one TV crew, a man with a bulky videocamera plodding glumly like a pack-camel behind a perky, sparrowish woman who carried a microphone and poked her head into every office she passed.

The odd thing about a press frenzy is the perverse illogic of it. Even if you were media-mad, you couldn't answer all those phone calls if you wanted to—unless you had decided to spend a big part of each day chatting with random strangers on the phone. The press probably figures (if it figures anything) that you will agree to a few requests and decline or ignore the rest, but human nature isn't like that. If someone asks you a question you answer it, but if thirty people bellow questions simultaneously you shrug and walk away—assuming you are not some kind of politician, and I am not. (Many of the press's problems might originate in the tendency to regard politicians as normal.) If you don't feel well, and people who are just home from long hospital stays rarely do, you are that much more likely to shrug the whole thing off, and conceivably it crosses your mind that your assailants are oblivious jerks.

This personal sense of grievance is unfair, up to a point. The twelfth caller inside of an hour doesn't know he is twelfth, and is just doing his job. Some messages even begin with pro forma apologies—"I'm sure you're getting loads of calls, but I work for the *Fluvial Gazette* and I'd like to ask you a few things; please get back to me at . . ." What emerges is a question that haunts this story of America and the press: If you do something bad not out of malice but moral sloppiness, does that make *you* bad? We tend to answer with a quick "of course not" and then bat the question away like a mosquito, because we hate talking about right and wrong, good and evil, insofar as those terms apply to particular human beings. We keep the ideas around for show. They are the fancy wedding cakes in the caterer's display-case freezer; they've been in there so long, no one has any idea how they might taste if you thawed them out. We are not judgmental. It is beyond some of us even to tell a child that his grammar is wrong. We catch the President behaving badly and he tells us "mistakes were made"; he is speaking for the whole nation. (We criticize the poor guy for not being judgmental enough, but haven't we told each other for years not to be judgmental *at all?*)

So the phone rings all the time, but we can't take it off the hook because many people actually need to reach us. We get an answering machine to screen calls—the machine picks up and broadcasts the caller's message as he is dictating. At the end of the day we have accumulated twenty or thirty or forty press messages, and there is no way we can go through all those either, not seriously, without dedicating the evening to it. So we erase them as fast as they accumulate, but the same characters keep calling. A TV producer wants me to call her immediately—she wants to send a crew to my home this afternoon. Next day she calls again with the same pitch. Next day again. It crosses your mind that not only are these people oblivious jerks, they are not too bright. Another grossly unfair conclusion, but there it is; I'm no paragon.

I might be sitting at the kitchen table during those last two weeks of August, my right hand propped on a pillow, practicing my painfully slow left-handed writing on a large pad I had once used for drawing, feeling as usual like hell, physically and mentally—and through a window across the room I notice, maybe, a TV crew in its station wagon creeping left to right across the top of my visual field. (Our front lawn slopes upward to the street.) I have my back to the rear deck and the reason we bought the house, the forest valley with the brook. The phone rings. My wife's deliberately information-free leave-a-message announcement, and then a hopeful, fruity woman's voice rings out in tones appropriate to coaxing a child (for we are all children in the press's eyes), letting me know which radio station I should please call at once. The station wagon creeps. The phone rings again. If I am extra-lucky the fax machine to my left comes to life and a reporter who has already faxed half a dozen messages faxes another. The message is complete; the phone rings again. The wagon turns round and creeps in the other direction. In the end you can only smile and accept the fact that, somehow or other, you have wound up inside a Fellini film.

But when you start paying attention to what these people are saying and writing, the smile goes away.

Some of my press encounters were simply annoying. There was a certain tendency, for example, to publish false information. All sorts of garbage found its way on air and into print. While I was still in the hospital, one newspaper broke the story that I couldn't wait to get back to my computer and log onto the net, whereupon I was planning to skulk around electronically and catch the criminal in no time. I never said or thought it; such an unspeakably idiotic assertion! Which of course jibed perfectly with my personality—I might as well have told people that the moment I got home, I was planning to dress up like Oprah and host my own talk show. One evening around the time Hut Man was arrested, my wife was on the phone with the FBI when I got home—they were checking whether it was true, as a local news outlet had just reported, that I had been arrested.

It must be the very first thing you learn in journalism school: Why do research when you can make things up? Thing number two: You are Nature's Noblemen and the peasants are dying to talk to you. So go ahead, give 'em a thrill. "I could explain what I'm after," said one TV producer's message, "but instead why don't you just give me a call and we'll chat?" Sure, I can't wait. We are awakened one morning before seven by a radio producer who was sorry to call so early, but she has already slotted me in for a rush-hour interview this morning and is calling to let me know.

The *New Yorker* decides to run a profile, and naturally you cooperate with a *New Yorker* profile—how does a small shovelful of dirt feel on being asked to lunch by Queen Elizabeth? So it comes about that I get a phone call late one afternoon from a staffer at the magazine. She identifies herself as the subeditor for (let me see if I can get this straight) fact pieces dealing with suet, gravel and minor provincial scientists. The profile will run next week, and the editors have decided that a certain self-portrait drawing ought to accompany it, so if I would please Fed-Ex the thing for delivery tomorrow morning. That is all. Is it crucial, I wanted to know, that you get the thing *tomorrow?* Yes it is crucial. So we throw together an emergency wrapping job and my wife tears out to a local office that closes at five, and they don't run the piece next week or any other week. Eventually the author reclaims it and it runs somewhere else. I feel safe in asserting that Harold Ross would never have put up with that sort of thing. (When someone finally offers me a trip in a time machine, I know exactly where I will go. The temptation to meet Leonardo or Shakespeare or Bach will be very great, but I am going to a certain small Chinese restaurant in lower Manhattan on the night, somewhere in the early '30s, that Ross and E. B. White took Ginger Rogers out to dinner.)

We are still in the funny-not-sinister region. What *is* sinister, and perverse, and leaves you deeply shaken, is the assumption in the news industry that a person wants to be addressed and treated as a "victim."

I referred earlier to the "victim culture"; many people agree that it is a bad thing. But it is also perverse—so unnatural it demands explanation. What bizarre tactless perversity could account for a person's believing that anyone would *want* to be called "victim"? Would *you* want to be known as the "Robbed-at-Knifepoint Kid"? "Mr. Skin Cancer"? "Mrs. Three Car Pileup"? All of us are unlucky somehow, sometime; many of us have suffered hard blows. Few of us are willing to see ourselves and our accomplishments blotted out by the word "victim." Not many of us will allow ourselves to be wrapped in a neat package with "victim" stamped on front. We don't deny or minimize the hard blows we have suffered, but neither do we allow them to define us. Our enemies don't define us, we refuse with outrage and disgust and contempt to allow them that privilege; we define ourselves. Most people who call you "victim" nowadays aren't doing it out of meanness, granted; they are aping other people's bad manners. Southerners who threw around the word "nigger" weren't necessarily doing it out of meanness either. Everyone else talked that way, so they did too. And that made it all right?

The victim culture is bad because it is demeaning and discouraging to people who are stamped "victim"; it fosters disastrously wrong training in our schools and colleges also. In many classrooms nowadays, students are taught to see society as a victimization machine and themselves (particularly if they are not white and male) as likely targets—tasty morsels unless they watch out. Victimization and discrimination are facts in our society and every other society, and it is our duty to fight them. And if a talented young woman (say) finds that someone won't take her seriously because she is a woman, that's unfair. She is entitled to call herself "victim" if she wants to. Of course, that she is talented is also unfair—and she will get all sorts of breaks on that account. In that respect she is an anti-victim, or whatever—it's too bad we don't even have a word for it. A word would help.

It goes without saying that everyone is a victim in some ways, lucky in others. Some of us get better deals and some get worse. Some of us get unbearable deals. But most of us can picture with no trouble at all a person who is worse off than we are. "Count your blessings" is a kindergarten-level moral insight, but nowadays we teach children to nurse their grievances instead. Why? It's perverse.

The painter known as Balthus once claimed that he had a greater need for a château than a common laborer does for a loaf of bread. On one level the statement is idiotic. Yet he wasn't clowning; he suffered real anguish on account of pro-aristocrat (or anti-commoner) discrimination in modern France. (He eventually fixed the problem by awarding himself a phony title and compelling people by force of will to take it seriously.) Nearly everyone has real sources of suffering that are imposed by society and are unfair. But in most cases you can take victimhood or leave it alone; the choice is yours. Dwelling on your unluckiness is a waste of time, savoring your victimhood gets you nowhere—and if we had any sense, that's what we would teach our children. Take it for granted, we would tell them, that each and every one of you will be offered the opportunity one day to call yourself "victim." When your big chance comes, turn it down.

A big New York TV personality has her staff fax me a bunch of letters and then (when, unaccountably, I'm still not interested) treats me to a fax over her own exalted signature—she simply cannot *imagine* what I must be going through. But she is bound and determined—it is a matter of simple *fairness!*—to make sure that for once, the *victims are heard!* It's her duty, dammit, and she intends to do what's right. I got hit with this spiel repeatedly. The victims deserve a chance to speak! The *victims*—that's your cue!—that's *you,* dope! I heard it from radio and TV people and editors and print reporters: they all want to talk to me because I am a victim. I faxed back a response to the TV personality, politely explaining (you start seething only when the same thing has happened again and again) why a person might not want to be dumped in the "victim" basket. I never heard back, but hadn't expected to; she was busy and had other, less ungrateful victims to patronize.

I would never have predicted it, but another aspect of her letter turned out to be commonplace also. She told me that she couldn't imagine what I must be going through. To my surprise, people kept saying this—with the best of intentions; there is nothing mean or callous about it. It isn't like calling someone "victim." But the phrase demonstrates something interesting about modern America. People used to sympathize in such terms as "I *can* imagine what you must be going through." Sympathy means suffering-along-with, after all. Not many people have been blown up by a mail bomb, but every adult has had experiences that give him emotional purchase on other people's misfortunes. But in modern America, victimhood is sacred. Literally sacred: set apart. When you approach the sacred victim, protocol requires *not* that you treat him as a fellow man but that you proclaim and honor his set-apartness.

———

By September the press storm is dying down; the odd gust still rattles the trees, but I can finally get my bearings. Interview requests filter in at a much-reduced rate, and if they are reasonable, I am willing to go ahead and be interviewed. But of course, relations with the press aren't only a matter of my own say-so.

A few weeks after I get home, Nick Carriero arrives with a high-quality printer, fast modem and some other electronic odds and ends for which the university has generously shelled out. Without further ado he hooks them up. (Goodness is a matter of seeing what is right and not offering to do it, just doing it. I learned this from my mother; it does no good to hear about it—you have to see it in action. It is a rare quality and I don't have it. Carriero does.) Chris Hatchell comes along as he will on many subsequent occasions to show me the mail, tell me what's happening and do anything he can. My home computer setup had been third-rate—I hadn't even owned a printer. I don't like electronic gadgets and have no tendency to accumulate them. But clearly I will be working from home a lot more from now on, and I badly need this equipment. I log on, tap out an e-mail message to my colleagues in the computer science department, and soon afterward it appears in the *Washington Post*.

The man who wrote that *Post* story turns out (ironically) to be a gentleman and a first-rate writer. My letter had been reposted by some unknown villain to a public bulletin board. The *Post* merely transferred it from one public forum to another, and I can't fault them for doing that.

But this is a common story nowadays. There was a conference call not long ago among the Speaker of the House and some colleagues, and one party used a cellular phone. Eavesdroppers in another state listened in on a scanner radio, recorded the conversation and gave it to a congressman. Somehow a major newspaper just happened to get hold of it and ran a front-page story headlined "Gingrich Is Heard Urging Tactics in Ethics Case." A better headline would have been "Is This Newspaper Listening In on Your Phone Conversations?" Subhead: "Sure, Why Not?"

But if you convey private information using e-mail or cellphones, people tell me, you get what is coming to you. It's a shame, but modern communication technology is insecure. Don't get all huffy about it.

The problem, however, is in our morals, not our technology. Old-fashioned paper correspondence was "insecure," yet protected anyhow—by law and decency. If you stumbled on someone else's letter, that didn't give you the right to steam it open. If it was open already, that didn't mean you could read it. And a person is far more likely to stumble on paper mail that is none of his business than e-mail or cellphone conversations; ordinarily you stumble on *those* because you are out looking for them, prospecting for burglary opportunities. But we are not judgmental, so we blame the technology and absolve the people.

The press experiences that went beyond funny and obnoxious into the realm of evil came later.

The major newsmagazine, for example, that called its cover story on the capture of the suspect "Mad Genius." But the evidence all pointed not to insane brilliance but sane stupidity. Madness is, of course, exculpatory, and nowadays people *do* commit murder and get away with it as a matter of course. I would have thought that designing and assembling a series of complicated machines, successfully deploying them to wound and kill people, authoring political tracts and sending them off to newspapers (can you *really* be a mad genius of a bomber but a sane fool of a writer?), eluding capture for years—that any one of those acts is proof *prima facie* that you are mentally competent. So why exactly did they call the suspect "mad"? Well, it seems he was bad at small talk. He was a slob and dogs hated him. He referred to himself in his letters not as "I" but (to quote from the article) using "the madman's we." In other words, if the writers had any evidence to support their claim, they forgot to put it in.

It could be that Hut Man *is* insane. I have no reason to think so but in the end I don't know, and the magazine writers didn't either. They just assumed he was: assumed that a man who killed three people with bombs had to be mad. And what if he had only killed one? If you merely hurt someone with a bomb, would you maybe be sane? Or does bomb-throwing make you a lunatic automatically—whereas stabbing somebody to death with a knife doesn't rule sanity out? In the end this is an argument for eliminating the very idea of guilt, and I can only guess that the attraction in calling a criminal "mad" is that it gets you off the hook and you don't have to be judgmental. But a society too squeamish to call evil by its right name has destroyed its first, best defense against cutthroats. Our best line of defense against crime is to hate it. Look at modern America and you see this at once: No free society can defeat crime by force. If we fight it (as we are doing) with force alone, it overwhelms us.

The press merely reflects elite opinion in society at large. But where does *People* magazine get the perversity to name "the Unabomber," this squalid cutthroat coward, one of the most fascinating people of 1996? I have been told that this is like *Time* naming Hitler man of the year in 1939, but it isn't. Hitler had millions of followers, had already reshaped Europe and established himself as a destroyer on a global scale. The bomber is merely mean and small. He had no ideas of consequence, killed at random, had no followers and reshaped nothing. What about the purveyor of news and gossip to a fancy clientele on the internet who rattled on about "Ted" the bomber, and the risk we run of misunderstanding him? When you have a personal link to the criminal's crimes, perversity like this hits you in the stomach and takes your breath away. It forces you to ask *what is wrong with us?* What makes us blur the line between good and evil and, in so doing, invite criminals to attack us and terrorists to kill our children? I found myself turning this question over night and day; I had no choice.

The worst piece of perversity I came across was an opinion piece by a journalist in a major newspaper which set my supposed views of technology side by side with the bomber's and compared them, a sort of Christian-versus-lion matchup for the amusement of Sunday readers. For good measure the author gives a false account of my views. I am "the pro-technology professor" according to him, but anyone who glanced at *Mirror Worlds* knew better before he reached page one. (The epigraph is two statements put together in counterpoint: the London actress Fanny Kemble enthusing over her first trip on a primitive railroad and John Ruskin denouncing the railroad, and technology in general: "There was always more in the world than men could see, walked they ever so slowly; they will see it no better for going fast.") This journalist's nuanced world view is the type that defines "wine" as "a colored liquid"— which, although it maybe doesn't capture everything that is *most* distinctive about wine, is nevertheless sharper than certain definitions a person might come up with, if he were tired, nervous and had been decapitated.

But the real problem here is far worse than simplemindedness. Arguably Hut Man's crimes turned his political opinions into news, and a journalist has a duty to report them. But this writer wasn't reporting opinions, he was trafficking in them. Explicating and exploring them, weaving them together with mine—he introduces one passage with the phrase "Where the two thinkers differ . . ."—laying them out neatly for inspection like fish on ice, selling newspapers, getting paid, pocketing the proceeds. I can imagine a phone call in the ICU as I'm struggling to figure out this world I have been plunged into—"I'd like to stage a little get-together," the voice on the telephone says; "you and the man who might easily have killed your children. You'll have a debate and we'll sell tickets, okay? No? Well you don't mind if I go ahead without you?" His piece is called "A Terrorist and His Target: A Debate Between the Unabomber and the Pro-Technology Professor."

No, he didn't actually phone me in the ICU or at any other time. But why is it that so many of us know in our stomachs that it is a filthy business to traffic with unrepentant murderers, even if no one ever told us? Why do we know without even thinking that we don't want to buy a watch (cheap!) from such a person, or sell him one, or invite him to dinner, or publish a respectful commentary on his political views? We know it because we hate what the murderer has done. We hate what he is. We could never dignify such a person by doing business with him. If we did, we would feel like dirt.

It is perverse of us as a nation to let newspapers publish this sort of thing without objecting, because it hurts us all. The only question is how much. It is in our interest as a society that crime should not pay. To keep it from paying is usually beyond us nowadays—people rob and steal and murder and get away with it. But the payoff this particular criminal sought (and it's the same with other terrorists) was attention for his ideas, in hopes of our dignifying them with serious discussion. It was up to us: Would crime pay or not? We thought it over and decided yes.

———

Where does our perversity come from? Our "don't be judgmental" perversity, our trafficking with murderers, our morally disastrous unwillingness to draw a sharp, hard line between good and evil? As a matter of fact, we know exactly where it comes from.

Have a look at some exhibits.

Back in 1957, Norman Mailer had a thought; does murder *really* justify a man's getting up on his high horse and acting judgmental? In his famous essay *The White Negro,* he looked on the bright side of two young thugs' murdering a shop owner. The piece was hugely influential. The 1974 French film *Going Places* treated "moral considerations of any kind," writes the film critic Stanley Kauffmann, "as irrelevant, encumbering, ridiculous." The movie was hugely influential. Intellectuals are against the making of judgments, no doubt about it. Is one culture better than another? One "lifestyle" or family structure superior to the rest? Hamlet a more interesting character than Batman? Search us. The president of Northwestern University considered a holocaust-denier on his faculty not long ago: "I believe his views are monstrous. But I don't want to set myself up as a censor of his views. Who decides what is distasteful?" *I don't want to set myself up as a censor*—that's exactly what the journalist must have thought who published the "Debate Between the Unabomber and the Pro-Technology Professor." How could a journalist set himself up as a censor of other people's views? Who decides what is distasteful?

"Don't be judgmental" is a perversity that originates, I believe, with intellectuals. (I will define the term later, but in essence intellectuals trade in ideas and have close ties to the modern university; in the first instance, their audience is mainly each other.) It's hardly surprising that intellectuals should oppose the making of judgments. In their world, tolerance is a cardinal virtue. In fact it comes pretty close to being the only virtue. Tolerance is good in itself. Unfortunately, people have accused intellectuals of another less attractive characteristic also, a lack of common sense. Such rednecks as George Orwell, for example—"one has to belong to the intelligentsia to believe things like that," Orwell once wrote; "no ordinary man could be such a fool." Loving tolerance is good, and lacking common sense is no big deal; mix them together and you get the moral equivalent of alcohol plus sleeping pills.

When I say "intellectuals" I don't mean *every* intellectual, of course. Some intellectuals are wise and kind and upstanding. But if you allow carpers to shoo you away from every generalization before you have time to explore it, you have no hope of coming to grips with basic questions about modern America.

So I claim that we picked up this perversity about "being judgmental" from the intelligentsia; but the relationship between intellectuals and the country at large goes much farther than that. America is radically different today from what it was at mid-century. The biggest changes started, people agree, somewhere around 1965. "The 1960s," the historian Paul Johnson writes, are "one of the most crucial decades in modern history, akin to the 1790s." "The last time I visited New York," wrote E. B. White in 1977, "it seemed to have suffered a personality change, as though it had a brain tumor as yet undetected." He reflected on New York City as it used to be before the Cultural Revolution: "The city I described has disappeared, and another city has emerged in its place—one that I'm not familiar with. But I remember the former one, with longing and with love." The perversity I want to understand starts in the '60s. What happened? This: intellectuals took over the elite.

They didn't set out to do it, it just happened. Two tectonic plates that used to float nowhere near each other collided, one rode up over the other and things have never been the same. What happened was a sort of coup. The nation's elite positions were mainly occupied by a certain class of person. Persons from a different class loomed up, jettisoned the old occupants and took over. It *had* to happen this way because, to a remarkable extent, we pump our elite class out of our prestige colleges and universities, and after World War II we turned those institutions upside down. The new elite is dominated by intellectuals and their trainees. The implications are vast.

Years ago the "New Class" theorists made a similar claim. They argued that the huge postwar expansion of college attendance had created a new class of intellectuals and their disciples, and that a power struggle between this new class and the old elite (whose champions were the leaders of the business world, for example) was changing the country. Time has passed, and where the New Class theorists saw a battleground, the battle today is over and the intellectuals have won. William F. Buckley once made the famous pronouncement that he would rather be ruled by the first two thousand names in the Boston phone book than the combined faculties of Harvard and MIT. Now that we *are* ruled by the combined faculties of Harvard and MIT, you can see what he meant.

My claim is big and sweeping, and maybe sounds far-fetched. But you see the evidence everywhere of rule by Intellectualized Elite.

Contemplate some interesting intellectual crowds: the poets, painters, writers and *salon*-keepers around the young Picasso in 1905 Paris, say—some of them Bohemians but some true-blue intellectuals, with theories to sell and ideas to put over. Or the Trotskyists around *Partisan Review* in 1930s New York. Or the Paris intellectuals of the 1950s—Sartre and Simone de Beauvoir, Genet and Beckett and the rest. There is scant love lost in any of these groups for organized religion, the military, social constraints on sexual behavior, traditional sex roles and family structures, formality or fancy dress or good manners, authority in general. Intellectuals have had these tendencies throughout the twentieth century, and back to the nineteenth and into the eighteenth. But illegitimacy didn't zoom up in 1905 Paris. No legal assault on public displays of religion took place in 1930s America. Nor did divorce rates explode or sexual constraints crack wide open or vulgarity become normal in popular culture; none of these things happened *until the intelligentsia took over.* And *then* they happened. It would be absurd to claim that intellectuals have imposed their tastes everywhere. But it is impossible to miss the obvious trend—the translucent, overlying tint that is thinner in some places, deeper in others.

What does it mean for society to be intellectualized? This: David Letterman interviews the actor Keven Kline on TV. Letterman has a question about one of Kline's movies in which "you play a Frenchman—French *person*," correcting himself. It is one of those moments when the ground fractures and you see straight to the core of modern America. Letterman is no intellectual, as far as I know, but he is part of the intellectualized elite and talks its language. We nearly all do nowadays.

That the "man" in "Frenchman," the "his" in "everyone took his seat" excludes females is ridiculous and the intelligentsia knows it. (Or knew it. In today's schoolroom the facts are suppressed on principle.) Let's assume that the indeterminate "man" and "he" reflected male dominance originally. Things had been otherwise for a long time when Eudora Welty wrote, in her 1984 memoirs, that "It is always vaunting, of course, to imagine yourself inside another person, but it is what a story writer does in every piece of work; it is his first step, and his last too." "*He* has lost all suggestion of maleness in these circumstances," notes E. B. White in the final, 1979 edition of *The Elements of Style*. "It has no pejorative connotation; it is never incorrect." But the intelligentsia had a point to make, and decided to wipe these usages out. (There is no conspiracy at work, just a congenial, like-minded group of decision makers.) "He" had to be "he or she," "mankind" had to be "humankind" and so forth. These words were repeated endlessly and in time— surprise!—they caught on.

Fine, humor them; who cares? But good prose had been wobbly on its feet to begin with, and this new decree was a punch in the guts. There is no stylistic rule more basic than "shed excess baggage, so you don't slow down the camel train." If you care about good writing you omit words that add no meaning, and prefer shorter to longer ones that mean the same thing. When your prose is lugging freight that has nothing to do with the topic and is only put there to register your support of feminism, the outcome is not merely ugly but ludicrous. It reads as if it were plastered with bumper stickers. Eudora Welty writes by ear: "When I write and the sound of it comes back to my ears, then I act to make my changes. I have always trusted this voice." The intelligentsia writes by the harsh light of ideology.

So here we have Letterman and Kline, and Kline happens to *be* a male, actually, and even if you had the nonsensical idea that "Frenchman" only means a french *male* Kline's character is nevertheless a Frenchman. But after decades of elite babbling, "man" is radioactive. Letterman uses the suffix and the moment it is out of his mouth, drops it instinctively, as if he had reached for a sandwich and come up with a rattlesnake. This is what it means for society to be intellectualized.

———

Tolerance is the modern intellectual's cardinal virtue. Why?

The American civil rights struggle of the '50s and '60s plays a special role among intellectuals. It is the basis of their religion, in the sense that the Passion is at the bottom of Christianity and the Exodus of Judaism. And the civil rights story is well suited to this sacred role. It has moving and compelling nobility, in fact combines certain aspects of the Exodus and the Passion. It is a plausible basis for a religion. As for Judaism and Christianity and the American civic religion, they never appealed much to the intelligentsia; by the late 1950s the bloom was off Marxism (which anyway never had the universal appeal among intellectuals that the Civil Rights religion would develop), and it was time for something new. The civil rights story built on themes that had long attracted intellectuals—a morally gross majority, an oppressed minority struggling for justice.

It all made sense. Yet the religion raised up on this basis did not. The Exodus was followed by the creation of morality at Sinai. The Passion followed a life given over to basic moral and spiritual questions. But the civil rights struggle wasn't preceded or followed by the creation of a comprehensive new moral framework. Intellectuals who flocked to the Civil Rights religion were left with a morality empty of any principle but tolerance—which is a good principle but not the only principle. There is truth also, for example. "Truth" has been roughed up by certain tough modern academics, who say that it is only a "social construct" and that "objective truth" is a fraud—and that's all well and good for truth, which is a pushover, but no professor is fool enough to mess around with "tolerance."

Civil rights religion provided the faithful with handy archetypes for angel and devil, righteous and wicked. Angels are beings who fight for tolerance. Devils fight against it. The average man doesn't qualify; he is merely righteous or wicked. The archetype of the wicked man is the average white American—or (as later amended) white American *male*. He doesn't sic dogs on civil rights marchers, but you can assume he is intolerant— although you hardly expect him to own up to the fact, and he may not even realize it himself. (Until recent decades this assumption was probably fair up to a point: Most white Americans probably were bigots, to some extent.) The archetype of the righteous man is the black American victim. When intellectuals or their minions call you "victim," they are awarding you an honorary connection to the powerless victimized black minority, and for all its bizarre perversity they mean it well.

———

This was an astonishingly different country before the intellectuals took over.

A museum in Peoria staged a show of "Dick and Jane" readers from the 1940s and '50s. The last edition was 1965. Throngs came—the show was held over—and people would look at the old books and cry. "Any time we had people crying in the galleries," said the Public Affairs Director, "we knew they were looking at Dick and Jane pictures." An odd scene for an art-and-science museum, where rocks and paintings don't ordinarily get that kind of rise. Especially strange because, as the experts point out, in those retrograde Dick and Jane books "mother cheerfully does the housework. Father wears a suit to work and on weekends mows the grass and washes the car . . ." The experts were stumped. But only temporarily: Of course, *everyone* feels nostalgic about his childhood, and nowadays '50s nostalgia is a fad. That's true, and so is this: People cry when they think about that lost era because in many ways, life was better then—

We know about the statistics that track the big social changes since the early 1960s, statistics on divorce, illegitimacy, fatherless households, educational attainment, crime. Here is just one: Today, one third of American babies are born out of wedlock. The intangibles cannot be tracked, but here is a glimpse of them. McSorley's Old Ale House was (still is) a famous saloon in an out-of-the-way corner of lower Manhattan. In 1939 it served men only. That year Marjorie Hillis published a New York guide "for the woman vacationist"; she mentions the handful of male-only New York bars and dismisses them in one parenthetical phrase: "probably pretty dull." The author Leo Rosten was hugely successful in the 1930s with a series of funny pieces about a Jewish immigrant named Hyman Kaplan. The jokes center on Kaplan and his fellow immigrants butchering the language in a night school English class.

In both cases we see a victimization offer that is tendered and turned down. Marjorie Hillis was perfectly entitled to outrage over McSorley's no-woman policy, but in the event she neither condones nor condemns it; she rises above it. Outrage against McSorley's isn't worth her time. New immigrants might have been outraged by Rosten—or *The New York Times* might have been, on their behalf. Instead, immigrants became his biggest fans. Those 1940 New Yorkers might strike us as cold and blasé; we would probably have struck them as infantile.

The country was far less powerful then, far less rich and far less sophisticated in medicine and science and technology. Important matters. On moral terms we have improved in one area, inevitably the one intellectuals care about: We are far less bigoted and more tolerant. In 1940 people were judgmental across the board, and we sometimes forget what that means: Whether you did something wrong or merely unconventional, society would jump on your back, and your only choices were to haul the weight around for the rest of your life or leave town. John Updike refers, in a recent story of Depression-era Pennsylvania, to the "power of righteousness and enforcement that radiated from the humorless miens of the central men." That power was designed to intimidate and it did. On the other hand, I mentioned McSorley's and Marjorie Hillis. Joseph Mitchell wrote up McSorley's in 1940 and noticed that the day's receipts were kept in a row of soup bowls and a rosewood cash box. Fear of stickups kept no one up nights. Marjorie Hillis says of New York that "I feel safer on its poorest streets than I do on a quiet country road." According to the *Londoner's Guide to New York* of 1936, "one may walk the streets for years without seeing anything more criminal than the solicitation of alms or the manifestations of inebriation." New York City had no street crime to speak of.

You see the difficulty and diciness of comparing past and present in a striking brief scene in *Stage Door*, a 1937 movie starring Ginger Rogers and Katharine Hepburn. They room together in a boardinghouse in Manhattan's theater district. Hepburn is newly arrived and rich. The other residents are poor. It's bedtime. Hepburn throws open a window; you hear the traffic rushing, streetcars clanging (there was a streetcar line on 42nd Street) and men shouting on the sidewalk. The million lightbulbs of a huge marquee across the street flash on and off. The room is a great pulsing rhythmic buzz. You need eyeshades to sleep. Hepburn remarks on the great atmosphere. She won't think it's so great, Ginger tells her, when the garbage trucks show up at five the next morning. If I were rich, Ginger says, "I'd scram out of here plenty fast, and leave you here with your atmosphere." She wants to get rich and get out. But Hepburn *is* rich and wants in. Lights flash, men shout, gauze curtains toss in the breeze and they go to sleep.

By 1937 standards, we are nearly all rich and have got out—have left behind the boardinghouses, the scratch-and-struggle for a living. We are well out of it: Ginger was right. If we moon after 1937 America we risk playing Hepburn's role—the rich import who sees only what is bright and charming because she is a slumming tourist. Except—so far as the movie is concerned, anyway—Hepburn and Rogers are both right. When Hepburn's character throws open the window, you see a relationship between city and citizen—an emotional entanglement—that we can barely imagine today. She is a girl in love. She and Rogers and the rest live right at the city's center: They are part of it, safe in it, lit up by its brilliant energy. You can't embrace Manhattan today the way Hepburn's character does (the way so many real people did, too), because the city, for all its remaining good points, is a psychopath and would kill you if you tried.

Your emotional entanglement with Manhattan or some other city or the country at large counted for a lot less, needless to say, than your actual-person romances. But it had this significant property: Normal romance turns you inward, away from the community; your romance with the city turned you outward and toward the community. The city-dashing, city-dazzling, city-as-person created emotional gravity that drew people and held them; there is no equivalent today. We float around weightless (grinning dimly as our toothpaste tubes drift away), each of us in his own separate solar system. "We have nothing binding us together," says the TV journalist Cokie Roberts; "no common ethnicity, history, religion or even language—except the Constitution and the institutions it created." Thanks for the news, but you needn't have bothered; you're stabbing a corpse. The intelligentsia has repeated this formula so persistently and so fervently that it has finally come true. Ridiculous, some people say: Why blame intellectuals for the fact that we are an immigrant nation and so, *of course,* have nothing but the Constitution to bind us? But the logic is false, and there is no *of course* about it. The first-generation Jews and Italians (say) of 1937 New York had no common history, religion or native language, and the idea that European-ness gave them a shared ethnicity would have struck them as idiotic. But in time they developed a shared history, shared language and shared American ethnicity. Of course, for all their poverty and hard times and wearying struggles, they did enjoy one big advantage over Mexican or Vietnamese arrivals today: no intellectualized elite hectoring them.

Set against our big gains in tolerance since 1940 are huge losses in the soundness of families and schools and cities and morals and morale. The safe conclusion is that we are strong where 1940 America was weak, and vice versa; 1940 is the foreign destination where the dentists are worse but the beaches are better.

Fair enough, yet there is more to the tolerance story than meets the eye. For example: Jews nowadays are evidently in the pink. They continue to earn like Episcopalians and vote like

Puerto Ricans (as political analysts say), and areas once closed to them are wide open. In 1940, American anti-Semitism was a significant part of Jewish life. So Jews are much better off today. Except that (inconveniently) Judaism itself is dying. More than half of American Jews marry Christians, and every religious branch except Orthodoxy is increasingly cut off from tradition and is suffocating: Tradition is oxygen to a religious community. Some people claim that American Judaism *had* to come apart when anti-Semitism ended—the community was a bursting suitcase, and you could hold it together only by sitting on it. Remove the hostile outside pressure and your suitcase is doomed. I don't believe that. The nation at large has turned its back on tradition and authority and family, and that is more than enough to account for Judaism's decline. In any case, Jews are better off in power and money terms than they were in 1940, and in certain respects they might even be better off morally and spiritually; in others, they are clearly worse off morally and spiritually. Which doesn't mean that there is anything to be said for anti-Semitism; merely that America's moral and spiritual fabric is unraveling, and Judaism is unraveling along with it.

Blacks would appear to be an open-and-shut case. In 1940 race prejudice was normal throughout society, and our treatment of blacks was a national disgrace. In the late 1990s race prejudice is gone from our laws and gone from our customs. But the black community has bifurcated: One part has prospered since the reforms that culminated in the late 1960s; the other part—the underclass in the slums—is worse off. Jews are more powerful and prosperous than they used to be; some blacks are too, and some are less. In both communities there has been a moral, spiritual and religious decline. There is nothing to be said for intolerance, but those are the facts. They are less clear-cut than we would like to believe.

Women are the most important case by far. Are women on the whole better or worse off than they were in 1940? Women are more important to the national climate than Jews or blacks because there are more of them, and every American who doesn't happen to be a woman is intimately connected with one or (at very least) used to be. The American basics boil down to motherhood and apple pie—everyone knows that. Apple pie is doing all right. I will turn to motherhood later.

I made up these theories the way a person scratches an itch, not with cool detachment but in order to solve a pressing personal problem. My analysis of modern U.S. culture in terms of a takeover by intellectuals is too overloaded with passion to resemble any normal, proper theory. It wasn't conjured up out of controlled field studies. It arose in circumstances that more closely resemble an interrogation toward the end of a detective novel, where the hero (namely *me*) has cornered a malefactor and is bullying him with a pistol into admitting where the girl is stashed or the best friend is locked in a closet. The theorizing was done under stress and the niceties were not observed. Maybe the whole thing is no good. All I know is that I found the lost persons where they were alleged to be, and the theory allowed me to make sense of my life. And for that reason I suspect it is mainly true. There are many reasons I wound up in computer science, for example, but an important one in retrospect is my dislike of intellectuals and my unwillingness to be one. I wanted a trade. I don't know if I really got one, but that was the idea. And within the university, technology is the least academic field. I love E. B. White not only as a brilliant writer but as a stubborn nonintellectual.

Whether American life was better overall in 1940 or better only in certain ways, as I moped on the sofa in fall '93 looking American degradation square in the eye because I couldn't help it—it was looking me square in the eye—1940 America was a soothing refuge, and I fled there.

Even if we didn't like birds anyway, which we do, I'd need some birdfeeders outside the window nearest the computer where I write, because the machine wedges constantly and takes five years to reboot—during which time birdwatching not only entertains me but counteracts my tendency to shout curses. (Because I am an expert at computing, I know exactly which parts of the machine to curse out.) In early November our birdfeeders are doing great business and tufted titmice are the leading customers. The tufted titmouse is a small gray-and-white bird that bears deep psychological scars on account of its ridiculous name but covers them up. Experts point out that *you would think* it is one of the cheerfulest birds around, which shows that it is in denial. Other animals know this, and their name for the unfortunate creature is "tufted denial bird."

I am a bird-lover from way back and once owned a profoundly antisocial parrot. But I only recently realized that I had the world's best birdfeeder site right here. The subtle ochre of goldfinches in winter, the grayish magenta of housefinches and rusty flush of sparrows and watery-orange dabs on the tufteds, the grayed red of winter cardinals and, best of all, the female cardinal (we have only one) with her deep-orange bill and soft olive-ochre feathers—they make up together one of the loveliest, moodiest scenes in nature.

CHAPTER FIVE

I

T'S MID-SEPTEMBER and I have been home about a month. I continue to spend much of my time sitting around in confusion. I also happen to be reading all sorts of books about 1930s and '40s America: rereading books I have around, asking my wife to fetch others. I am just doing it, for (I imagine at first) no special reason. In fact there is a book I badly want to write and I am getting ready to do it, preparing in my shambling, sleepwalking way, unawares. The whole period fascinates me, but my interest centers on the 1939 New York World's Fair, an event that perfectly embodies the whole dead age.

The requisitions mount: books, old magazines, videotapes. My wife visits used book, antique and ephemera dealers with lists I have given her. Chris Hatchell starts an endless round of visits to the Yale libraries to find books. When the word gets out that I am working on this period, I start hearing from people. Friends of my parents who visited the Fair dispatch packages of memorabilia. It turns out that there are dealers around the country who specialize in world's fair literature and ephemera. My sister puts me in touch with one and buys me a 1939 *Official Guide*—as objects go, the best present I ever got. The dealers have lists of material and the names of other dealers. The project starts running into money. I find the topic enthralling but am still not exactly sure what the purpose is.

(Some people have the impression that any showy and violent misadventure automatically makes you rich—if you can make a fortune on coffee burns at McDonald's, imagine what a bomb must be worth!—but unfortunately it doesn't work that way. I might in principle have sued Yale for something or other. I have no idea whether I would have had a case, but the country is lousy with contingency-fee lawyers who will take on this sort of thing for a percentage of the proceeds. To spin the wheel costs you nothing and you could strike it rich. The only problem is, the bomb wasn't Yale's fault; and after I was injured, the university did everything it could. It's tough when your obvious deep-pockets legal target behaves impeccably and bears no moral responsibility for your problems in the first place, but what can you do? Grin and bear it.)

At Yale, the fall term is already under way. Back in the hospital I had promised to teach as usual in the fall. When I got home I repeated the promise. But as September started, it was clear I couldn't do it. Couldn't even in principle—I was spending too many hours at the doctor's. But teaching would have been unthinkable in any case. I felt too rotten even to contemplate it.

In mid-September I promise to be back on the job for the spring term, but my confidence is dropping fast. As I sit on the sofa with the rods sticking out of my wrist, my hand hurting (at times acutely) and my arm hurting, my chest hurting and itching (at times maddeningly), my vision blurred, my energy

zero and my confusion great, standing in front of a classroom
is an act I can't even imagine. It has a nightmarish implausibil-
ity, like wandering onstage at Carnegie Hall in your pajamas.
But if I can't teach in the spring, I will have to admit that my
life has been knocked off the rails a lot more decisively than I
have let on.

We need some work done on our phones. The repairman
presents himself and I show him where the problem is. He sets
to work. Then he turns round suddenly and asks, "Are *you* the
guy who got hurt by the mail bomb?" The name must have
seemed vaguely familiar and I had, Lord knows, a shambling,
wounded look, not to mention the rods sticking out of my
arm. That's me, I tell him. "Wow," he says, "what can I say?"
His intent is to convey sympathy and he succeeds. But I can
only share his bafflement. I look at myself and ask constantly
"What can I say?" I am overwhelmed one morning with a sense
of tragedy as I pass my older boy's bedroom and realize how I
used to know all the junk in every corner of it, and spend time
in there every day, and nowadays never go in; it is foreign territory to me. Stifling tragedy—for a while I can't even move; it's
absurd, but rationality doesn't enter into it.

Of the hours I spend at doctors' or clinics (with my wife beside
me the whole time), physical therapy accounts for the biggest
slice. Several mornings a week I see a therapist who is working
on my shoulder, arm and hand, Marcia Dymarczyck. She had
been on duty in the hospital too, making a million splints and
(among other things) imparting the secret of how to stand up
without fainting, which I can assure you comes in handy. (You
pump your legs in a certain way when you stand up, to get the
blood flowing uphill.) Fall '93 has a physical therapy flavor.

Marcia is a tidy, smiling, energy-packed woman with dark hair and a white lab coat who seems for all the world to be crazy about physical therapy—as if she enjoys having morose, damaged people presenting themselves for treatment all day long, which on the face of it is pretty unlikely. A lady who *liked* doing physical therapy would presumably slip outside and smash her head against a wall for recreation. But Marcia is too sane for that, so her behavior is probably just a case of excessive resourcefulness and good cheer. "Hello hello hello!" she says when I come in with my wife, because her energy level is too high for just one hello.

The clinic is a sunny L-shaped room. The vinyl upholstery runs to loud orange. The staff is all-female and operates at a brisk bustle. It's cheerful—sort of. Except that the bare polished floor and shiny instruments give it a cold hospital indifference and the feel of death. But there happens to be a receptionist out front who has a musical Spanish name and looks like Carmen is supposed to in Bizet's opera, but never does. She has a mysterious, teasing smile for even the broken-downest wreck of a patient. Now and then she saunters back to the clinic in her elegant dark suit and dark stockings and crimson lipstick and heels (close your eyes and it's 1946: wa-*waa* of the sax, the headline in two-inch block letters, EXTRA: GORGEOUS DAME STOPS TIME), and the room's sinister shininess is canceled out for ninety seconds as she chats with a therapist about scheduling. Then she saunters out and the ambience glazes over again, a chilling smile.

There is a big operation scheduled for the end of September: wrist rods to come out, busted ear to get stitched. Until then, there is not much Marcia can do. It's not clear what my hand will be like after the operation or how I will feel or what I will be able to do. It *is* clear that the rods are getting more painful and driving me crazy.

Surgery day got to be a routine: wake up early, can't eat, go to the hospital, hang around; the hours under anesthesia drop out of your life. When you wake up confused and wildly thirsty you are a crazed rat racing round a cage you can't get out of. What is this? What's going on? You try to figure out what's happening and they give you an ice chip. Your thoughts settle, gradually, like the white sparkles in a shook-up snow dome. I take badly to anesthesia. Maybe it's just that I have never gone in for naps.

They are not supposed to admit wives to the recovery room, but when they admit mine, I have an easier time coming to. At length they wheel you to a room, you spend a night and go home. So October is under way. My ear has been fixed and for days after the earache is monumental. I sit on the living room sofa and watch newsreels from the 1940s—with no plan in view; for no particular reason.

One rainy night in the Late Earache Period our fax machine whirs into action. Some fellow in California has a request: Would I please fax back immediately a list of fifteen books similar to my own most recent one. He is specific about the fifteen—but forgets to include directions in the event I am only able to come up with (say) twelve. Writers hear from crackpots all the time. It is part of being a writer. It is also part of being a crackpot. The non-crackpot letters amply make up for the others—many are interesting; some are moving, and remind you that writing is not the completely pointless obsession you often suspect it is.

But the FBI manhunt puts all crackpot letters in a new light. With a killer on the loose, the unexpected coming-to of the fax machine on a stormy night is ominous. What's that noise? Listen carefully: The storm has the house surrounded—drumming the roof, tapping the windows, applauding in the trees—and yes it is a fax: You can just make out the machine's faint intermittent mouse-scratchings. A fax at this time of night? You walk into the other room, switch on a light and wade through shadows to the far wall where a strange letter is emerging line by line. We call Ron. We are in constant touch with the FBI. We call them, they call us. Over the long months between the day I am hurt and the day Hut Man is captured, we turn over a truckload of crackpot letters and faxes and e-mail.

In the period after you have been hurt by a mail bomb, all inbound communication channels are radioactive, and you look at the strange message on curling fax paper in the shadows as if it, too, might start hissing and explode.

There is huge manhunt on. It is said to be the largest and most expensive hunt for a serial criminal in U.S. history. The FBI has set up an 800 number for tips and will log 20,000 calls before the man is captured. Two hundred suspects come under investigation, they say, at one time or other; but that is the official number, and I imagine that unofficially they looked at thousands or maybe tens of thousands. FBI men pop up constantly with questions. They are working hard.

After the bombings in June, people thought that a break might be imminent, that somehow or other the criminal might have tipped his hand. But it is becoming clear that no break is imminent. Life with the bomber on the loose is a condition to be got used to. Life with a modified body is a condition to be got used to.

The FBI had a brainstorm (some faction of the FBI did, anyhow): By means of extensive interviews with all the bombing targets and correlation of the results, much could be learned about the bomber's identity. Suppose it turned out, for example, that at some point in his life every target had published a comic opera disparaging to Norwegians—you can see what I'm driving at. They called this approach "victimology." I thought it was silly, but was admittedly biased against it as soon as I heard the name. Still, I patiently answered the questions. And to be fair, when they got their man, he was exactly what the FBI had predicted he would be: a white middle-aged male weirdo acting alone.

Ron comes by my office at some point highly excited. Without his regulation suit and tie— it's that important that he come right over and see me. So here he is in a polo shirt and— *jeans?* My memory must be faulty here. We talk for an hour; I wish I could be more helpful, but there is little I can offer on this occasion. He leaves and his idea goes nowhere. And once again I am impressed by his seriousness and intensity, and the FBI's. This endless, exhaustive manhunt is a bad business. The worst kind of frustrating hard work, the kind where you can't sit back and leave it alone for a while, because the result could be more people maimed or dead. Maybe a child, next time, will lose a hand or an eye, or bleed to death. Maybe a mother will get blown to bits. So the FBI agents work hard constantly, turn up leads, get excited about the leads, pour gigantic effort into proving out the leads—and wash the leads out; and onward to more leads.

It is mid-October when I finally stumble on the mother lode of cool. It takes the form of late Beethoven string quartets.

These October days have a slow oscillating rhythm imposed

by drugs and pain, like a buoy's rise and fall in a rolling sea. I wake up feeling rotten and take painkillers and feel somewhat better. The painkillers wear off hours before I can take another dose. Those hours are bad and pass slowly. Finally the moment arrives when I can take more. I feel somewhat better, and exhausted: Pain is exhausting, and the painkillers themselves are mildly sedating. I wander off into a free-floating mental state that isn't sleep but is something like it: eyes open, mind adrift. Then the drugs wear off and the cycle repeats. Monotonous up-and-down rhythm. The rhythm traps me; I am living the rhythm instead of life. When I am at home and not at a medical appointment, I read my 1930s books aimlessly (anyway it feels aimless), or watch old newsreels, or listen aimlessly to music.

Occasionally I practice left-handed writing or log on to my computer at Yale. I send some e-mail, but it is a while before I can work up the energy to read any. I haven't read e-mail since the morning of the explosion. Thousands of messages are waiting, and the system has all the appeal of a flypaper that has trapped so many creatures it's disgusting. The very first message is labeled "explosion in Watson," the computer science building. A late-breaking news item circulated to many people. I don't much feel like reading it. And, of course, I have to type with one hand. I used to be the world's fastest typist, more or less. If I am saddest when I contemplate the things I can't do with my boys, and my old paintings, I am bitterest when I struggle to type.

I had always loved the late Beethoven quartets but hadn't paid much attention to them in recent years, partly on account of an intense obsession earlier in life. Around mid-October I start listening again, because of a craving for violin music. I had studied violin as a child, rising to the exalted status of concertmaster of my elementary school orchestra (which may not have been the worst orchestra in history, but was probably the worst up to that point) before retiring to devote myself wholeheartedly to goofing around, and piano on the side. But somehow I have convinced myself this fall, at least when I am asleep and dreaming, that I can return to the violin—you do all the fingerwork with your left hand after all, except for pizzicato.

In reality your grip on the bow and the way you move it are crucial, and there is no chance of my ever playing the violin again. But this fall it is therapeutic for me to believe otherwise and I do, knowing the whole time that the belief is false. (The mind is capable of amazing tricks.) I can't bring myself to listen to piano music but crave violin music. One day in October I return to the late quartets, starting with mankind's greatest musical achievement, the *Grosse Fuge*—and as I sit wearily and aimlessly on the livingroom sofa listening, the music begins to shepherd my chaotic thoughts back together again.

An explanation of these quartets' magical power would take dozens of pages (and might fail even at that), so I will simply make an assertion and move on—Beethoven's music has no emotional content. None of it does, except for the beautiful and weirdly anomalous last movement of the *Tempest* sonata. Music without emotional content feels cool to the touch, and I desperately need cool. The late quartets are more intense than anything else Beethoven wrote—and for that reason they feel cooler than anything else in music; anyway, they do to me. You get the sensation listening to this music that you have staggered out of a hot, smoky, drunken, noisy saloon onto an arctic plain where you wander in amazement under high bright stars.

One afternoon I am listening to the last movement of the C-sharp minor quartet—it has a stupendous climax, a mere sequence of modified scales in dotted rhythm in which the earth shatters, followed by a strange unraveling conclusion where the remains dissipate like smoke; and suddenly I find that I am aware of the backyard and the fall. The white wooden rocking chairs on the deck I had ordered a few days before I was hurt and never sat in. The big oak, urn-shaped like an elm, and smaller trees around it with the stream passing below. Coming out of a long daze. Quiet, grateful relief: the child waking from a nightmare to find his bedroom just as it is supposed to be, and his parents down the hall.

And as I listen to Beethoven quartets, the purpose of the 1930s stuff finally comes clear. I have a book in mind about the 1939 New York World's Fair. Part novel, part history. The project is a decisive turnabout in my life.

The explosion stopped me dead with a staggering jolt. But such an event is not all bad. It makes you face the fact that life is short, things change, you die. As I sit in the dark livingroom that October, it finally dawns on me that I have to turn the vessel around right now or die unhappy. I'd imagined that when the time came I could pull off a supple turn like a stunt pilot, but in fact (which should have been obvious) as you get a family and build a career, your life grows into an aircraft carrier, and turning it becomes steadily harder. Coming to a dead halt may be a necessary part of making the turn.

With my 1939 book, which was part fiction and part literary essay and had nothing to do with computers, I started off in a new direction. And I found as I started to move again that I had shaken off every tendency to care about other people's evaluation of my career and life's work. Regarding anyone's general feelings as to whether a computer science professor could really be *serious* about painting or writing (and many people do have strong feelings on the topic), I couldn't care less. There is nothing pretty about my newfound arrogance; it is cold and dismissive, and also lifesaving, and I don't know that I could have achieved it otherwise than the way I did.

So Beethoven cools me down. That doesn't mean I am happy that October; I am not. But after a season in hell, plain, ordinary sadness is a condition to treasure.

CHAPTER SIX

JOHN MARKOFF published a story about me in *The New York Times* around this time saying that in general I was all right but suffered "bouts of depression." The word I had actually used was not "depression" but "discouragement." Markoff is another member of my small band of honorable reporters, and if writing "depressed" instead of "discouraged" is the worst mistake he ever makes, he is a lot more punctilious than I. Yet there is a world of difference between discouragement and depression. Depression is a pathological state. If it's bad enough, physicians can treat it. Discouragement is a moral state, a failure of heart; you treat it by taking courage, not Prozac.

Markoff has a charming little-boy smile and the shaggy, endearing manner of the type of sheepdog that makes a big hit in children's movies. You only deduce he is a reporter from indirect clues, such as the fact that, however many nosy personal questions you ask him, you know exactly as much afterward as you did before. *He* on the other hand knows everything. His curiosity about technology is ravenous. And when he recounts technology tales a marveling note comes into his voice, and a spellbinding rush of enthusiasm.

He had published an article about me before, in early 1992, which may have a role in this story. He had intended for the article to focus on *Mirror Worlds,* which was just out, but somehow it wound up in the Sunday business section instead of the magazine, and the editorial climate over there favored a more practical topic. So the piece was rejiggered and came out focused on our "parallel programming" research instead. In parallel programming you aim many computers at one big problem simultaneously in order to solve it fast. The parallel programming technique that Nick Carriero and I had developed was seeing a fair amount of real-world use, which made it a legitimate business section topic.

Several years before today's internet-based Web-world first emerged, *Mirror Worlds* forecast a computing environment that is a lot like the Web but more powerful. Had the *Times* editors gone with the original *Mirror Worlds* focus, they would have looked prescient in retrospect. Anyway, they didn't. (And in fairness, no one looks at a newspaper in retrospect.) But they did give the refocused story big play, with a billboard-size photo on the biz-section front page in which I am standing at a blackboard looking like a mad scientist.

Now Hut Man as we know reads the *Times,* and he might have got interested in me, Markoff hypothesized, on account of this big, splashy Markoff story. After all, the country is full of technologists, and even allowing for the Harvard factor there are plenty just at Yale. How come my dossier rose to the top? I think Markoff felt badly about this, as if in some indirect way he were responsible for the crime—which of course he was not and couldn't possibly have been. A reporter can't temper his writing to the anticipated outrage of any group of readers, least of all the bomber-mathematicians. Who can say what might provoke such as Hut Man, and who cares? Here is a man whose life's work is the creation of misery. To adjust your own work to his whims is not only impossible but morally unthinkable.

But discouragement is not depression. I have achieved melancholy and am ready to move on.

Markoff points to a wider issue. Roughly a year ago I was praising a *Washington Post* article to a friend—an article about me; I didn't love every word, but it was vigorous and fair and well written and well done—and he asked me, "How come you hate the press so much in general and love all these guys in particular?" Or words to that effect. I told him that I'd rather hate people in general and like them in particular than *vice versa* in the manner of so many famous idealists. But that wasn't the point. People such as Schwartz at the *Post*, Markoff at the *Times*, Levy at *Newsweek*, Barlow at the *Hartford Courant* wrote about me the same way they write about all sorts of things, with intelligence and fairness and judiciousness and decency. And they are all members of the press in good standing. Yes I do believe that the press in general reflects the moral confusion and degradation of U.S. society, and has gravely hurt us all. But that doesn't mean there are no fine journalists. It's not as simple as that.

My claim about the intellectuals taking over is complicated also. The moral world they have built, in which tolerance is the only unquestioned good, is wrong and unacceptable. But that doesn't alter the rightness of tolerance itself.

My post-bomb experience wasn't simple either. My disgust at the press sent me crashing through cultural swamplands for months and years, searching frantically for an answer to the all-important question: What has gone wrong with this country? On the other hand my family and friends, the FBI and hundreds of the medical people I encountered were magnificent, and people all over the country sent their best wishes for no reason other than plain decency and fellow-feeling.

The country is going to hell but its people are not. Its elite leaders have failed it—but if they succeeded in the past, why should they be failing today? Because today's elite is not yesterday's; when the intellectuals took over, everything changed.

I am asked sometimes whether I am an optimist who thinks the country is getting better or a pessimist who thinks it is getting worse. (Debating this question is a favorite party game among conservatives.) I think it is getting worse, and am also an optimist. I'm not convinced I will see any big improvement in the cultural climate within my lifetime, but I know for certain that in the long term, one will come.

Crime rates have dropped recently in big cities, especially New York, and the streets are cleaner, and in some ways the urban climate has improved. It would be stupid to belittle those gains. They are important. I hope they continue. But our crime rates remain barbaric by 1940 standards. I work in the city of New Haven, where crime is also said to have decreased, and I negotiate every day the constricted world crime has created. Moving around the city we are captains piloting our vessels through dangerous shoals. I have two young children in school, and my wife and I struggle daily with an education culture that leaves crucial information out and puts nonsense and the occasional outright lie in its place. Just one family's experience, of course. But here is one devastating piece of evidence among millions that speak of the collapse of U.S. education: The number of parents who have removed their children from the schools altogether continues to grow. Today roughly 1,200,000 school-age children are educated at home, more than New Jersey enrolls in its whole public school system. On the complete battery of standardized exams, home-schooled children average 37 points higher than public school children. Average spending per child at home is $546 a year, versus $5,325 a year in the public schools (excluding the cost of home or schoolhouse). The huge performance gap between black and white public school pupils on reading and math tests dwindles or vanishes among home-schooled children. Obviously the home-schooled children have certain big advantages: dedicated parents, dedicated teachers, private attention. But that 37-point gap is astonishing. If you saw a gap of that order between home-doctoring and professional physicians, you would draw the obvious conclusion: that the medical "profession" is quackery and no profession at all.

Things are bad, and on the whole they are getting worse. And yet American culture and the American nation have strengths that are unparalleled in history; no other culture so fundamentally strong, generous and big-hearted has ever existed, and you can count on Americans coming through in the end.

———

So the press story is complex, and many related stories are complicated too. Most complex of all is the underlying question—are we better off today, or were things better on balance at mid-century, before the Cultural Revolution? In the end there is no answer, but the question is important anyway. And we can't take it up seriously without considering the biggest, most fundamental difference between 1950 America and today: relations between man and woman, parent and child.

The country has changed in many ways, but these changes are deepest of all. A little over a year ago an acquaintance informed me (intending it just as an observation, not an accusation) that I was "an extreme right-winger." I don't think of myself in those terms; I asked him why he said so. Because you believe, he told me, that society is better off—other things being equal—if mothers stay home and rear their children than if they get jobs. The conversation took place shortly after I had published an article in *Commentary* laying out that claim.

I was flabbergasted by the idea that this belief about motherhood made me an "extreme right-winger." But as I thought it over, I had to concede that it probably did. I doubt there is a single elected official anywhere in the country who would endorse my contention. Maybe some politicians believe it, but to say so would be political suicide. (It's generally agreed that Pat Buchanan is the farthest-right politician with any national constituency; he once made a statement something like mine, but then retracted it.)

In 1950 you would have been hard put to find any Democrat or Republican who did *not* endorse it. And it isn't merely that Americans used to believe in traditional motherhood; they used to believe in it strongly. You might have got the impression that they built their whole framework of social beliefs on top of it. Nowhere else have we wiped the slate clean so decisively inside of two generations. Whether you like the change or not, it is so dramatic it demands explanation.

You cannot account for it unless you accept that a revolution has taken place. You might like the revolution or not, but there is no way to deny the fact of it.

The tendency has developed in recent years to describe the United States as a "feminized" nation. Clearly the feminists have had their way. Yet imagine that you are a selfish young man of twenty-one and it's 1960. How could the country be fixed up to make you happier? We could set things up (first things first) so your girlfriend won't give you such a hard time when you want her to sleep with you. (We'll just arrange for the schools, churches and community to take it for granted that she wants to.) If you get her pregnant, why not abortion-on-whim? But let's say we abolish shotgun weddings also, just to be on the safe side. Once you're married, we'll get rid of this business about supporting your wife. She can bloody well support herself. And as for kids, they're adaptable, and we'll raise up a professional childcare establishment to murmur reassuringly about daycare and motherless afternoons at home being just what the doctor ordered—great for your kids and great fun, too. Kids or not, a man wants to move on, so divorce will be easy and alimony will be gone. A perversity of historic proportions: Feminists have helped create a utopia for loutish males.

Early 1997, NBC news reporting from the University of Michigan: "Dating takes a lot of time," a male senior explains, "it costs a lot of money and also I think out of the little time that you have, you want to kind of maximize what you get out of it." So he follows the usual campus practice: join a group at a bar, get drunk, go home with a girl who is also drunk and shrug her off the next morning. "They never call; you never hear from them again," a female student reports. This is plain old ordinary precivilized male behavior. What's new is, nowadays the women pitch in. Presumably they are egalitarians and have no romantic notions. "Women will sleep with men the first night, randomly," according to a female senior; "I really don't see why men feel the need to date." Evidently they don't feel the need to date. "Dating," claims the NBC reporter, is "a practice which on this campus and others is history." (NBC adds this interesting note: "One-third of the students' parents are divorced.")

Modern feminism may have had perverse consequences, but we *needed* it, so that women would have opportunities this intolerant nation had long denied them—right? But here is Betty Friedan writing in 1963 that "all professions are finally open to women," thanks to the "removal of all the legal, political, economic and educational barriers" that used to bar the door. Friedan is cited by F. Carolyn Graglia in a remarkable 1996 essay. From the day she announced her intention to become a lawyer, Graglia writes, "until I left my law firm in 1959 to raise a family, my aspirations were never questioned—not by the teachers and counselors who helped me obtain scholarships, nor by the employers and colleagues who always supported my career. I was a woman, and I was a lawyer, and there was an end of it." "The only disdain I have ever experienced," Graglia adds, "has come from contemporary feminists."* Maybe I forgot to mention that intellectuals hate to be judgmental except if you disagree with them.

From Graglia's point of view, modern feminism is an attack of some women upon other women. Those who read her article (everyone in the country ought to read it) may wind up convinced or not, but no one will dare call her opinions any less "authentic" than Gloria Steinem's or Hillary Clinton's. (In reading various cool and cogent women who reject one aspect or other of orthodox feminism—Graglia or Florence King,

---

*F. Carolyn Graglia, "The Breaking of the 'Women's Pact,'" *Weekly Standard*, November 11, 1996, 29ff.

Kate O'Beirne or Wendy Shalit, Mona Charen, Sally Satel—I don't understand where a person would get the nerve to call any one of them "inauthentic.")

Feminism has had perverse consequences; its assumptions are perverse too. That *men* were the biggest gainers when society expected mothers to stay home, keep house and rear children is laughable. Pop quiz: What have men traditionally wanted most? (a) A stable, orderly and emotionally secure household. (b) The best possible upbringing for their children. (c) Cash. Men leapt at the chance to send their wives to work.

Modern feminism is the most disastrous consequence of the civil rights religion. Leading feminists cast women in the black victim role, men as the bigoted white oppressors. The analogy is breathtaking in its perversity and gall. Throughout most of history, the typical white had no contact with any black except as boss, colonizer, conqueror or enslaver. And the typical man was closer to some woman than to any man. "Am I not better to you," asks the bewildered Elkanah of his barren, grieving wife in the First Book of Samuel, "than *ten* sons?"—her grief of course being his; and obviously not all marriages are any good, and men do hurt women, and the strong do hurt the weak; but a country that will swallow this ugly analogy that so belittles black suffering, is so demeaning to husbands and wives, mothers and sons, fathers and daughters—such a nation would swallow damned near any lie whatsoever. Where do we get this perversity?

But the whole thing fits tragically with the ascendance of the intelligentsia. Women intellectuals aren't known for their love of homemaking. Fine, who cares? Let 'em do what they want. In 1960 (as Graglia and others point out) loads of mothers worked; and in 1960 the careers they wanted, as Betty Friedan points out in effect, were largely open to them. *Of course* some men were nasty or belittling or boorish to working mothers in 1960, but nasty and belittling and boorish men are a fact of life. (The idea we are pursuing nowadays, that you can eliminate boorishness by making it illegal, is—what else can you say?—a typical brainstorm of the intelligentsia.) They *had* jobs, but feminists weren't satisfied; every other woman had to get one too. So they opened fire on homemakers with a savagery that still echoes throughout our culture. A housewife is a "parasite," Friedan writes; such women are "less than fully human" insofar as they "have never known a commitment to an idea." (These quotations are, again, from Graglia.) Helen Gurley Brown on the housewife, 1965: "a parasite, a dependent, a scrounger, a sponger." Gloria Steinem on housewives, 1970: "dependent creatures who are still children."

Now, fathers in 1960 loved their children as they do today, and were no more sentimental than they are nowadays about childrearing. But in 1960 relatively few fathers dared to bully their wives into taking jobs if the wives wanted to spend their time at home with the children. Nowadays such bullying is the norm; the usual mode of operating is to make it clear that you naturally *assume* your wife wants to work, and agree with her that any mother who doesn't is a sissy. In 1960 society accommodated mothers who wanted to work and rushed to the side of those who did not—*they* were the ones who needed aid and comfort and protection. Husbands have always valued the concrete benefits of cash over the intangibles of home life and the best possible rearing of children. Wives have always been driven to accommodate their husbands. Peace at home has always mattered more to women than to men, has always been mainly their business to maintain. Men have always been bullies. This society we have built lines up with the bullies. Of all the Victim Culture's sad consequences, this is the most ironic and the saddest.

Maybe we *are* unfair to homemakers, but in 1960 the cards were stacked against working women, and we are just evening the score, carrying out a bit of affirmative action sneering—what about that? Graglia doesn't buy it; my childhood memories don't support it. Young children of my generation knew with perfect certainty that Eleanor Roosevelt was the most admirable person in the world. (Later, Golda Meir took over the role.) The authorities I dealt with—teachers, librarians, the pediatrician—were mainly working women. I focused early on literature and art; there weren't a lot of women in art, but every second writer you heard about was female, from Agatha Christie to Margaret Mead. Most women stayed home. But only a moron would have concluded that women *had* to stay home, that staying home was the only respectable course.

Nowadays you will hear on *Sesame Street,* that obnoxious flagship of elite childrearing, about mothers in every conceivable line of work but homemaking. A few years ago, the eight girls in a local nursery school class were asked what they wanted to be when they grew up. One out of eight said "mother." Some people were shocked that even one did. A lesbian activist gets more respect nowadays than a homemaker. Whether a stripper or a housewife gets more respect is hard to say, but if she is unmarried and supporting an illegitimate child the stripper wins, no contest. A U.S. citizen of 1940—man or woman, black or white, Jew or gentile, left, right or center—would have found this state of affairs not just astounding but evil, and desperately perverse, and would have been even more astounded that no prominent person condemns it. "Where are the priests, ministers, rabbis?" he'd have wanted to know.

"Where are the newspaper columnists and editorialists, the top judges, politicians and business leaders, the university presidents, the public school authorities? Are they all *dead?*" No, but they are nearly all intellectuals, or trained by intellectuals; and you see the outcome.

You hear the argument sometimes that the motherhood revolution comes down to money: Mothers go to work because they have to, can't afford not to. Obviously this is true for single mothers, whose numbers have increased tragically since 1960. So far as married women are concerned, the claim is true in some cases but absurd in general. We are far richer today than we were in 1965, when far fewer mothers worked. Americans throughout the post-1965 years have been significantly richer than ever before in history. Back in 1935, average incomes were a small fraction of what they are today, yet the proportion of working mothers was under a third what it is now—families coped with hard times in other ways or made do with less. From the the end of World War II through the early 1950s real wages fell as prices exploded—but the proportion of working mothers merely crept upward. The sustained surge of the Motherhood Revolution didn't start until the boom years of the late '60s and early '70s.

But we all know who led the Motherhood Revolution: not mothers who needed money to put bread on the table but female intellectuals, who chose to work for the same reason they always *had* chosen to work, because they had interesting jobs and set no great store by the rearing of children. But in this country the intellectuals have turned upside down, the average working mother doesn't edit a literary quarterly or run the advertising department at a technology startup or build interesting cases at a high-powered law firm or produce documentaries for PBS. The Motherhood Revolution was an elite revolution and those are elite occupations. The average working mother sits at her desk in a big noisy room with a hundred other women at some insurance company in Peoria, and worries about her children. A generation ago she would have been at home taking care of them. Are we better off as a society now that she spends her day processing claims instead?

CHAPTER SEVEN

IN EARLY NOVEMBER I am still spending hours every week at medical appointments, and listening to music, and accumulating a growing pile of 1930s material like a squirrel hoarding very expensive acorns. But at last things are moving. I am working on my book. The idea of teaching in January is still daunting but seems progressively less ridiculous. In physical therapy I am making progress.

In the clinic several hours a week I sit at a small table, my wife beside me, and Marcia stretches and pounds and folds and bends my strange approximation of a wrist and hand, and I stare moodily into space (am still unable to look at the hand) with the occasional grimace of pain as appropriate. She builds an assortment of weird-looking splints that are strapped on for the night; they stretch out the muscles, struts, guy-wires and internal neuromuscular slinkies, which badly need stretching. But all the surgery has made it necessary to have more surgery, to clean up internal scars; and there is more work to be done on the fingers. Next operation, December.

Sometime in November comes a remarkable development: As a result of Marcia's efforts, I can unbend my right index finger and actually use it to type on a computer keyboard! It is the least damaged of the remaining right fingers; one segment got rearranged a bit, that's all. But at first I couldn't move it, and it was screaming pain to touch. With this right index finger back in play, my typing is revolutionized. It is nowhere near what it had been, but is a lot better. I am making progress.

Every morning after breakfast I take out the large pad and fill a page or two with left-handed writing. My letters are barely legible, and ugly to boot. They have a graceless, crumpled look, as if they were dry-clean-only and someone had tossed them in the wash. But I *am* making (creeping-slow) progress.

In December Marcia presents me with a device she has made—a rigid fake thumb that straps onto the remains of my right hand. Clumsily and uncertainly I use the right hand to grasp a pen, a thing I had never expected to do again. The shaft slopes at a strange angle and I have just barely got hold of it, but she plunks down a sheet of paper in front of me and I cover it immediately with drawings. The chance to recapture a piece of life I thought was gone affects me powerfully—but I haven't quite nabbed it; it flickers like a butterfly nearby but out of reach. This first construction of hers is too clumsy for serious use and too uncomfortable to wear except in spurts.

But further developments come fast, and before long a different device—a kind of handstrap originally designed for arthritics—allows me to draw again with my right hand. The handstrap cramped my style. Roughly a year later I'd progressed so much that I could draw and paint with my *left* hand. But despite its imperfections I set to work drawing and painting with the handstrap, unreeling with frantically intense effort a series of pictures I'd had in mind for years, clear on the fact that I never would or could stop painting again.

The literary aspects of my new book have been propelling me smartly forward. The miraculous fact that I can paint again kicks in like a turbocharger.

Not that everything is wonderful. My physical state remains pretty bad, and I am still worried about the oncoming start of the term. I am pinned up with strong painkillers to a normal life but I sag between doses. My blurred vision bothers me enormously; you feel as if you are bundled in window screening, or some other stuff you can see through but remain aware of. The screen not only affects your view, it separates you from the world. There are times when the out there turns into mere babble, and you feel agitated and put-upon and bitter and need to close your eyes, breathe slowly and let things settle. It's worst in crowds, and a class is a crowd. I was never crazy about crowds to begin with. Or, for that matter, classes. So I worry about teaching, am still uncomfortable most of the time and have lots more surgery ahead.

And despite this amazing fact that I am now devoting myself mainly to art—painting and writing—art is no picnic and never has been. At any rate, not for me. I am a stumbling clumsy oaf of an artist, a Keystone Kop, disregarding the brambles as I lunge after a private butterfly that grazed me once on the cheek (or maybe I dreamt it); I have a certain technical facility, but facility is as likely to be an enemy as a friend. It's a frustrating chase. I chase in prose or poetry the way I grab a big brush or a small one as I try frantically to pin down the painting I have in mind. My world view lines up wrong with the normal categories; I care about beautiful things and my range is narrow, but I am interested in a certain type of beauty instead of a certain type of thing. In paint one time, prose another, it's all the same desperate chase. Success is just as fleeting and the trail just as hard everywhere, and you are the same bloody wreck at the end of the day.

As the year ends I impress people as more grim than cheerful, except when I am with my boys. (It is around this time that I start telling them stories again—breakfast stories at first, because my energy runs down fast during the day.) But writing and painting propel me forward, and as I read and think and accumulate stuff, a third energy source roars into play: 1940 America itself.

When you make a direct connection between yourself and this America of two generations ago, the energy hits you with a jolt. Electroshock therapy. "The pedestrian finds it pleasant to stroll at the Fair," says the World's Fair Guide, "where the walks are of bituminous asphalt." *Asphalt,* the rubbery-hot smell and black sheen of it when you lay the stuff down: progress, the triumphant vanquishing of discouragement and mud. The sentence speaks with authority. Doesn't clown around or snicker or tongue-in-cheek-it as a modern guide would. You can hear the voice wavering between top-hatted suavity and the child racing in breathless with a great report card—the characteristic two-note birdsong of the world's fair. Even footpaths are worth contemplating and can be made better. Asphalt is wonderful—and so is black rubber for modern tires, and vivid golden-yellow plastic for radio cases, and streamlined armchairs framed in slick, bright tubes of chrome. An exciting era in transportation where you take nothing for granted, everything gets better including footpaths, and even after the Hindenburg has fallen blazing out of the sky, the memory of silver zeppelins aloft in zero gravity over Manhattan is still fresh—gigantic (the biggest were nearly *Titanic*-size—imagine a great ocean liner over-

head), gliding like divers who keep going long afte
cut into the water.

Writing, painting and a direct electrical connecti
are bringing me back. The energy that drives me
Toward the end of *Mirror Worlds* I have my pro-tec
ter ego explain to the antitechnology guy why you w
search in technology and what "scientific progress"

> Did you ever ride at the front of a New York City
> when you were a kid, looking out the front windo
> car roars down the track—rocking, screeching
> careening around the corners? With the blue tunn
> batting past? Remember the first time you rode in
> and it started barreling down the runway? Re
> running, when you were a kid, just for the hell o
> for fun? *That's progress.* Progress *means* the thril
> tion. That is: transformed childhood joy. That's w
> technology . . .

I used to approach many things on this basis, but
The energy driving me now is not the sort that powe
ward to adventure, it is the sort that presses you
desperate to make it in time. The march is no fun a
and on, but it is a lot better than sitting on your re
in a field someplace.

———

My friends were surprised, some of them, when I th
with a frantic intensity that has yet to abate into pa
it is the oldest strand in my personal history. I can't
a time before I was avid to draw, and I was convince(
artistic hot stuff by age six at the latest, at which

way from the field in a children's drawing competition on an ocean liner to Europe. We lived in Geneva for seven months while my father visited CERN, the European physics lab on the France–Switzerland border. He is a nuclear physicist by training, but his mid-1950s dissertation was part of the first wave to rely heavily on computers. He moved into computer science, a field he helped invent, and in the late '50s built one of the world's first artificial intelligence programs—developing in the process ideas that the field still relies on. Does my father's being in computer science have anything to do with my wandering into the field also? Of course.

I won a tall cardboard box of caramel candies in my shipboard triumph, which I generously shared with my younger brother after my mother forced me to. It was clear that art paid. As a child I loved Raoul Dufy's paintings and imitated them. When I first saw Matisse's *Jazz* I went crazy and churned out a pile of Matissean cutouts. My parents let me choose a print from an enormous, dusty collection in a Manhattan store, and I settled on a marvelous blue-toned Tintoretto study, which presided over my childhood as I otherwise devoted myself to baseball and assembling plastic car models at breakneck speed, never stinting on cement.

I took art lessons, as a child, with a talented woman who had an automatic garage door opener. They were rare luxuries back then, but her husband was an orthodontist. As a teenager I was a heavy user of the Metropolitan Museum in Manhattan. We lived on Long Island and I commuted by rail. I had fixed on Degas, where I am still fixed, and doggedly copied his paintings in pencil and charcoal. I was dogged also in copying Michelangelo drawings out of a Dover paperback. De Kooning, in a show at the Museum of Modern Art when I was thirteen, bowled the first whacking-great strike of my artistic adoles-

cence. The pins are still scattered; the smack-crash still resounds. As a college student I submitted a portfolio and got myself admitted to some sort of invitation-only drawing studio, to prove I could do it, and then with ostentatious undergraduate disdain declined to enroll. Didn't want my originality tampered with, I explained, and didn't believe anyone on the faculty could teach me a damned thing anyway. Acting out once again the Apotheosis of the Undergraduate, a role that could have been written for me. I atoned after graduating by assiduous work in life drawing classes at the Art Students League and the Ninety-second Street Y in Manhattan. But after a couple of decades of feeling stupid for my undergraduate behavior, I am no longer certain I did the wrong thing.

Life drawing is the basis of art. Whatever you do, in the end you cannot do it properly unless you have come to some understanding with the human figure. An artist needs to work with models throughout his career (anyway, I do), and people (anyway, some) have an uncanny willingness to pose—even when their faces won't make it into the picture. Vanity is not the issue. And posing is a zero-enjoyment activity; there are methods of being executed that are more fun. What it is, at least in part, is a widespread primal sympathy for art. When a model cares about painting, she makes a contribution to the finished product (women are more likely candidates) that amounts almost to co-authoring it. Joseph Mitchell writes about a fishing boat captain in Stonington, Connecticut, who took up oil painting and was good at it. You might have guessed that his hard-boiled fellow captains would have laughed at the idea, but they didn't—as of 1947, more than fifty of them had commissioned paintings of their boats. "Draggers, trawlers, mackerel seiners, and lobster boats." The price was $35 for local men, $75 for out-of-towners. Man and art have deep connections, though nowadays we barely notice them.

———

In late December and early January I assemble material for my class and feel as if I am approaching a parachute jump; I am aboard the troop plane heading to the drop site, and there is no turning back no matter how queasy I feel. I can't write class notes, so I type them on the computer. Can't write legibly on the blackboard, so am planning a seminar-style class around a table, although there will be too many people for a seminar. Class meetings last an hour and a quarter, twice a week—a modest schedule, except that I can picture myself keeling over after a half-hour of teaching. But here I am on board; no turning back. A few more weeks and Geronimo.

I have never taught this class before. I cooked it up last year before I got hurt. The goal is to teach some of the basics of computer science to nonscience students seriously rather than in the usual cutesy, patronizing way. Teaching science to art minds. But the way we usually understand it, the whole distinction between science minds and art minds is a myth. The intellectual world and the Bronx Zoo each have two entrances; people who enter by the woodsy birdhouse way see the Zoo very differently from ones who come in near the Asia department at the far end, with its lotus leaves and camel rides. The two groups approach the same buildings from opposite sides. If they give up easily, the birdhouse people may never reach Asia at all, and *vice versa*. But it's all one zoo. And art minds are capable of mastering the same intellectual territory as science minds, they merely approach it differently—speaking as an art mind in a scientific trade.

So my plan for the course is to visit scientific landmarks (like

Goedel's incompleteness theorem, Turing's work on the theoretical basis of computing, the ongoing battles over artificial intelligence) with a class of intelligent art minds in tow. That is a hard assignment, particularly if you are no great shakes as a teacher. Why I had to cook the thing up in the first place isn't entirely clear to me this December. Teaching a course I had taught before would have been a lot easier to cope with under the circumstances. But I forgot to account for the possibility, in laying the class out last year, that I might get blown up in the interim.

The course was to have another important component also, a survey and assessment of opinions on technology and science. Computers have done a lot of good and have also done a lot of harm, not in themselves (obviously) but insofar as they underline some of our worst tendencies. When they started to show up in force early in the 1980s, U.S. society was already infatuated with the phony Kool-Aid champagne of glitzy marketing and fancy graphics and shallow slickness. Our schools had already become tolerant, and preferred to graduate ignoramuses who felt good about themselves than decently knowledgeable proto-citizens who had occasionally been forced to work hard. Computers sent the slickness culture into orbit. A child's tendency is to "surf" the Internet and every other form of computerized information, slipping and sliding over the surface and never going deeply into anything. Pictures make the words look boring, videos make the pictures boring, multimedia extravaganzas make the videos boring. Who wants to put the time and imagination into reading a book when you can point, click and have fun with your brain on autopilot?

Technology in general has done society a lot of good, and the sky is blue. Technology has also brought about harm—mainly because we find it so hard to speak up for the status quo, even when the status quo is pretty good. A world in which children read books and listen to the radio is better than a world in which children watch TV. (That fishing boat captain Joseph Mitchell wrote up hated school and dropped out as soon as he could. What he did for entertainment as a boy was, the captain says, "read Frank books. Oh, Jesus, I enjoyed Frank books. They were called the Gun Boat Series. There was 'Frank on a Gun Boat,' 'Frank before Vicksburg' . . .") When children relied on books for entertainment, the United States was a more literate and sophisticated society than it is today. We switched over to a TV society; no one forced us to, and some people had misgivings. But there was no established school of opinion you could rally round that said, "This radio-book-movie world we've got is pretty good and has a lot of advantages, so let's keep it." Appreciating what is good in the here-and-now is one of the hardest feats known to man. Traveling by train was better than traveling by plane; it took longer but was a lot more pleasant. But no serious school of opinion defended train travel; there were a few railroad enthusiasts, who were regarded as slightly strange and probably were, and the trains disappeared.

The Motherhood Revolution centers on the same phenomenon in a vastly more important sphere. The 1960 status quo, where most mothers had the time and the means to attend to their children if they wanted to, was a high-water mark unique in history. And by and large the public seemed happy enough. (*Life* magazine, early '57: "Americans greeted 1957 with high-decibel revelry and effervescent optimism. The old year that was ticking away had been a very good one. . . . The year to come looked just as good or even better.") People liked the status quo, but they took it for granted and rarely put themselves out to defend it. When the onslaught came, American culture was a sitting duck.

Because of a trauma-induced cataract my vision is getting worse, and I am at the brink of the Eye Surgery Age. The ideal way to end the year? More hand surgery, of course. My wife reads me my draft manuscript as I wait to be wheeled into the operating room. It is never a pleasant scene: The stretchers stack up sometimes like incoming flights at La Guardia, and anxiety hormones eat holes in your stomach. Still, there is nothing that bucks a man up like his own words. This time I emerge with more wires sticking out of my fingers. They will come out in a couple of weeks, just in time for the start of the term. It's an annoying thing, having wires sticking out of your fingers.

It is time to start asking what I will do about my partial hand in the long run. A bizarre procedure has been developed in which a toe is grafted in place of a missing thumb, but I am not a candidate because too much of the hand is gone. Perhaps it's just as well. Some outfit in Manhattan specializes in fake hands made of plastic that you wear like gloves; they are so amazingly lifelike no one can tell you are wearing one. But I don't want a fake hand for decoration, I want it to use, and am content to cover it with a glove that looks like a glove. Anyway, the fake-hand option strikes me as grotesque, and wearing it would have felt wrong—would have felt like a let's-pretend game I don't have the heart to play.

Somehow I work up the courage to look at my hand.

I can type two-handed and paint again, and I think I will be able to teach again. As I gradually recover the means to do the things I used to, the reconstructed skills are unlike the old versions. They are dark and clumsy and usually somewhat painful:

reflections in dead black water of my old life. But I am lucky to be making progress. There is one other big skill I need to recover: must be able to drive again. I am counting on it. I used to love driving; read the leading car magazines every month. Had aspired since boyhood to own a high-class car. Now I aspire to drive my old Honda to work and back. Without a car our house might as well be located on the Great Steppe of Outer Mongolia, where at least our property taxes would be lower, because there is nothing you can reach on foot from this house-in-the-forest except more forest. Until I can drive again I am trapped, and other people will have to shuttle me everywhere. To drive I will have to be able to steady the wheel with my right hand as I do other business with my left. Will also need to feel halfway decent and muster enough energy to pay attention to the road. It will be a year before it all comes together, but my progress is encouraging, and I am willing to bet that the day will come.

———

The new wires come out. It is mid-January, and the first meeting of my class feels like a press conference. Mobbed and noisy. Cameras flashing from the far corners. Students cluster round as I make for the desk in front—could we ask you a few questions? Sit in? Take your picture? Do an interview? Yale's student journalists are frighteningly lifelike facsimiles of the real thing. But of course people are curious. Do I look strange, sound strange? Will I hold together? By virtue of getting blown up I have become a campus celebrity, and my disinclination to be interviewed adds a Greta Garbo notoriety to boot. The crowd is no surprise, but I still don't like it.

My right hand and wrist are covered by a surgical sleeve, my normal way of going around until I finally acquire a proper thumbpiece and glove. I am wearing my standard mental-patient getup with a sports coat on top. I'm nervous. More cameras flash. I close my eyes.

But when I finally go ahead, it's okay. The emergency fuel reserves a man can draw on when he goes forward despite not wanting to, not feeling he even can—they are amazing. They are among the finest design coups in the whole dazzling piece of work. I still draw on them today whenever I have to teach or lecture. Of course when you draw down your emergency supplies, you collapse afterward. Luckily I have a sofa in my office to collapse onto. I'd got it three years ago at a time when our newborn was keeping us up nights.

After teaching I am beat for the rest of the day, but even so it looks as if the term will turn out all right. A colleague whose office is just down the hall lives near us in Woodbridge, and she shuttles me faithfully to work and back. That winter it snows like crazy—the stormiest winter in memory. She's not fond of driving in the snow (who is?) but drives me through one blizzard after another until we feel like Peary and Amundsen. Through snow and ice she delivers me every time, reliability one hundred percent. It looks as if the term will be all right.

At some point that winter, I even cheer up. I was obsessed with *Swing Time*—it dates from 1936; of the Astaire–Rogers movies, it has the greatest dancing. Ginger sings a little number to Fred telling him that, when he is feeling downhearted, he ought to pick himself up, brush himself off and start all over again. Not Jerome Kern's greatest achievement, sounds too much like an advertising jingle, but it's catchy. Then comes an amazing dance and, later in the film, another. Astaire can dance without moving his feet. At the heart of this solo he merely stands with hips cocked, arms raised, his hands moving in the slightest, stiffest motion to the beat. If American culture has a dead center, this is it—unless it's the piano's entrance in Gersh-win's piano concerto, or the last couple of lines of the *Rhapsody in Blue*, or a Stuart Davis painting called *Swing Landscape;* there is a list of candidates, but it's not long.

I loved those dances and they bucked me up considerably, but when you get down to it, it was Ginger Rogers suggesting that I pick myself up, brush myself off and start all over again that did it. Not high art but a song that is very close to trite, performed with great style by a pretty girl backed up by the vi-brant, brassy noise of U.S. culture as it used to be. That winter I couldn't get the song out of my mind, but it was a couple of years before I made any connection between the lyric and my life. Obtuseness is my middle name.

———

Nowdays I have finally grasped a proposition that seems obvi-ous: that a writer has a duty to say what is wrong about life in his country and a duty, also, to say what is right. When the sta-tus quo is good you had better defend it, or you will wake up one morning and it will be gone. After the muddy turmoil of culture analysis, that is the message that rises like Ophelia's gar-land to the surface; and the same message, strangely enough, is the one you take away from the experience of surviving a mail bomb. E. B. White once published an essay called "What Do Our Hearts Treasure?" He got the title from a recitation his granddaughter gave at a Christmas play. The writing shows White's characteristic combination of sweet and dry—Amon-tillado, Madeira, the finest stuff; he and his wife find them-selves exiled for their health from Maine to Florida at Christmas time. They are unhappy but make the best of it. A package arrives from a daughter-in-law with photos of their grandchildren and the fragrant branch of a balsam fir, which had "unquestionably been whacked from a tree in the woods behind our son's house in Maine." They are happy to have the package. And that's the whole story. What do our hearts treasure?

In the sunlight of an early Sunday morning in November, my boys and I admire the frost-glitter on the brown crumpled leaves. We walk carefully downhill toward the brook—the frost makes for slippery going. Across the street to the pond; mallards stop here in spring, stay a few weeks and clear out in response to the inevitable job offer from a large firm in Manhattan, or whatever draws a mallard—and that leaves us still scanning the pond hopefully in November wishing for their return, because nothing dresses up a pond like a duck. The water surface is taut in the cold air, the reflection sharply focused: bare upside-down trees reaching downward into sky. We return to our yard and watch the chickadees in the big rangy juniper, the winged tulip tree seeds helicoptering downward, the tentative icicles reaching from casually tumbled branches toward the surface of the brook, which is running fast as if attempting to warm itself by exercise. A puny, sheltered Japanese maple has kept its crimson leaves; with their backs to the sun they are stained glass. There is a particular flower we visit often, a purple-pinkish, daisy-style chrysanthemum that hangs on though every other flower in the neighborhood has thrown in the towel. We admire (my boys and I) its spirit. It is the most spirited flower we have seen in a long time.

Because I am one of those tiresome moralizing types of father, I tell my boys I expect them to hang on like the flower, but with better hopes of long-range success. I cite for them often my favorite sentence from the Torah, do not follow a multitude to do evil. I'm old-fashioned, but I don't mind it; I tell them in essence what I was taught myself, and what my parents and grandparents were taught.

Had she stayed on the job and not quit to rear our boys, my wife would have been a superb architect. She could have made a superior surgeon also, or done beautifully in any number of other fields, but I am grateful that she didn't. Rearing two children and adding emotional wholeness to the world is an achievement that is incomparably more important than any surgeon's or artist's or scientist's. I am all for mothers working if they want to—out of selfishness if nothing else. My experience just with the medical system in the last three years would have been immeasurably more awful without them. Like most men I would sooner be surrounded by women than men on the job, and everywhere else. Some of my best friends (honest to God) are working mothers, or working mothers-to-be. I wouldn't hurt them for the world; how they live is none of my business and I don't begrudge them their high standing with *Sesame Street* and their fellow citizens; what angers me is a housewife's low standing. But when a working mother like the First Lady condescends (as she did in her infamous remarks about not staying home to bake cookies) to women like my grandmothers and my mother and my wife, I am furious and despise her. Not every career woman is snide and condescending, but too often the most prominent ones are. What sets my mother and my wife apart from these arrogant, preening women is not less strength or brains but more character. The axioms of modern feminism are insulting to the very people I have the greatest duty and desire to defend, and it should be obvious to anyone, whether he likes my position or hates it, that it would be gutless and contemptible of me not to fight

modern feminism tooth and nail, as hard as I can, however little I may accomplish. And I teach my boys to do the same.

Yet in many ways the status quo is fine and noble. Back in
1940 you could never tell why housewives did what they did,
whether it was devotion or just momentum. But today you
know exactly why homemakers do it: out of love. Some of their
families can easily forgo the second income, some cannot; but
every one of them could improve her standing in society by
taking a job. So today you can see these stubborn women for
what they are, the moral backbone of the country. A country
with this kind of backbone can't be such a terrible place and is
probably capable of weathering anything, in the end.

CHAPTER EIGHT

A YEAR LATER. The end of winter '95—late February, I think. We drive to the local discount warehouse to buy me a watch. My wife drives to the store but *I* drive our dreadful Scandinavian tub-stationwagon home. I am finally a driver again. It is a day of patchy snow and soaked pavement and the ground muddy, torn-up and tired; the vast parking lot is mainly empty and has a low-rent look, and the store itself, with its big blank façade, could be a state prison. A stiff breeze drives the clouds, and the sunshine is poignant and without warmth.

Not long before I was hurt, I had driven to this same store from my office in midday—to buy a watch. My old one was broken. By chance my wife was shopping in the same place. I was about to buy a plain, straightforward little number, but she convinced me that something a bit fancier was called for. I was a fine grown-up fellow, after all, and shouldn't dress like an undergraduate. I liked that fancyish watch, but it got blown up. At last the time had come to buy a replacement. Shopping is different this time around; I have to wear the thing on my right wrist because I can fasten it only with my left hand. My right wrist is several sizes larger than my left (although it is still within normal range); the watch needs a leather strap so I can avoid slipping a closed band over my injured hand. We find something reasonable and I drive home. Events of the last few weeks before I was hurt have acquired a painful numinous vividness; I picture myself in those final days lighter than air.

But it's good that I can drive again. I used to prefer a manual transmission but will never shift for myself again—though I can't help thinking wistfully, from time to time, how nice it would be to import a right-driving British car—something along the lines of an Aston Martin DB7 Volante might be okay. Luckily my old Honda has an automatic transmission.

(It wouldn't have had if I had got my way originally. I had tried before we got married to teach my wife to drive a stick-shift car. The lessons were memorable and had many good results, not including my wife's learning how to drive a stick-shift car—but she looked lovely in the low-slung driver's seat of my old Honda Prelude, which showed her elegant long legs to good advantage. She is capable of operating any machine on earth, but in the event, manual transmissions struck her as so hilarious she couldn't concentrate, and neither could I. The frantic lurching effect when you released the clutch suddenly with a playful snap, the bizarre layout of the gears—first up there, reverse down here, second over there—why would anyone design a car like that except as a joke? Why not just drive the thing straight to the nearest large museum and allow it to take its natural place in the Hall of Ancient Transportation? I described glowingly the aesthetic thrills of cars and driving, but I might as well have been talking about liverwurst. So when we got married and bought a new car, it had an automatic transmission. That car is my old Honda, and thanks to the automatic I can drive it.)

Early in 1995 the day comes, at last, when I have to admit it: *1939* is finished. One of the sadder days of my life.

Then a Saturday in late spring: I am sitting out back on the deck at my parents' house on Long Island, on a lounge chair, with my eyes closed. Pretty tired. A truck pulls up with a delivery. A couple of minutes later my wife materializes out back with my first copy of the book. Some kind of circle is closed. The energy is still pressing, but now that my book is done I have no sail to catch it, although I have yet to reach the place I am headed.

That summer *Newsweek* does a story about a certain hundred Americans who constitute, symbolize or somehow embody the "overclass" of hot-shots who lord it over the country, a project they probably cribbed verbatim from *A Thousand Great Rainy-day Ideas for Getting Everybody to Hate You.* I am one of the hundred. I am obsessed at the moment, I tell the interviewer, since she happens to ask, with the artistic possibilities of nonfiction. Lots of other people are obsessed too. No literary issue is more important. She asks something else in closing, and it comes up that I have thought, some, about software for subways. All references to prose, literature and art are instantaneously expunged, and I am described as the nice fellow who got blown up by a bomb and is hard at work on software for subways. Why this qualified me for the "overclass" I never found out, but it was nice of them to put me in.

Recently a prominent author published a piece about terrorism and identified me as the "computer wizard." It might be all right to be a computer wizard; I wouldn't know. In the last few years I have published *1939* and more than a dozen short pieces (some in magazines where this author has also published), mainly about art, one on architecture, one on movies, several on modern American culture. But to the world at large, science and technology are a strange, exotic locale: Leopard Island at the zoo. Where low-slung creatures pace balefully. Once you are there you are there forever, and the moat is not for leaping. The "wizard" epithet is flattering of course, and no harm was intended. You can only shrug.

That summer of '95, on the other hand—two hands are useful—our younger boy had just joined the older one taking piano lessons. He asked me one day whether, seeing that his favorite piece of music was the prelude at the very start of Bach's *Well-Tempered Clavier,* I would please show him how to play it. I had never heard of a five-year-old or anyone else having this monumentally austere steel bridge of a composition as his favorite. It is revered more than loved, even allowing for the trace of wistfulness toward the end. But I knew that it really was his favorite: He'd asked to hear recordings of it again and again. This was the first time he had ever wanted to learn any particular piece, and the one he had chosen was so simple and spare I was actually able to play it for him one-handed, with only a bit of smudging and faking. He wasn't able to play it yet himself, but he watched me carefully and learned a little. You never know when the sun will strike through the clouds and halt you in sheer amazement.

Young boys are not self-practicing, and my wife is an able pianist, so the job of sitting beside them and running them through their paces is all hers. Infrequently I substitute on a guest-appearance basis, standing behind them shouting orders like a basketball coach. They understand that I can't play any more, but for all they know, I might have been Rubinstein.

The week after the Oklahoma City bombing, the summer of '95, there was a big break in the case. Hut Man's goal was to be the country's number one criminal; he'd been described as the "most wanted killer" in the nation and was obviously flattered. But Oklahoma City bumped him out of first place, so he got to work. Within a week he had put another bomb in the mail, which killed the president of the California Forestry Association. After Epstein and I were hurt, the remaining two bomb attacks were both fatal. For us it had been a near thing. The bastard was getting better. I got that letter from him the same day the California bomb went off. He was desperate to get back in the news. Soon after, he wrote the *San Francisco Chronicle* that he was planning to blow up a plane out of Los Angeles, so air travel went crazy. And then his final big move: He orders *The New York Times* and the *Washington Post* to publish his 35,000-word political tract, plus regular bulletins thereafter so the public will always be up to date on his latest inspirations. If they agree, he will stop killing people.

It was a tough call for the newspapers. To say yes would be giving in to terrorism, and for all they knew he was lying anyway. On the other hand, to say yes might stop the killing. There was also a chance someone would read the tract and get a hunch about the author; and that is exactly what happened. The suspect's brother read it, and it rang a bell.

I would have told them not to publish. I'm glad they didn't ask me. I guess.

As soon as the tract materialized (the newspapers were still agonizing), the FBI brought it round for me to see. I didn't want to read it, but had an obligation to; I might conceivably pick up the subtle echo of something I had written or said, or a hint of some other kind. I hated like hell to read it. I hated to have it in my hands. And I didn't notice anything, unfortunately, except that the author was a tedious fool.

Next spring, the FBI finally got their man. They moved earlier than they had wanted to, because CBS leaked word of the stakeout—which might have ruined everything, I suppose, but first things first.

It was the spring of '96 at the start of Passover. You don't go singing in the streets at this sort of news, it's more like a toothache going away, but we were greatly relieved. The same victim-crazy reporters and producers I had scrupulously ignored many times before turned out again, but luckily it didn't occur to them that Jews sometimes spend the beginning of Passover with relatives out of town. The general belief among the bright lights of the news business, I am told, was that I had gone into hiding—possibly (I suppose) in a cave near a mountaintop on one of the craggy peaks surrounding New Haven, where I fought off eagles and shot a bear every morning so I could have bear-on-toast for breakfast. Yale students, I am told, were offered money to lead reporters to my lair. But that is only hearsay, and if I were the editor of a local newspaper my scruples would forbid my using it on the front page, except under a fairly modest headline.

Though many aspects of the plan may change, it looks as if the federal courts will try the accused bomber starting in the fall of 1997. I will testify. I have been receiving delegations for some time—federal prosecutors and their assistants, often accompanied by FBI men. Their goal is to understand my story in meticulous detail and to let me know what to expect as the legal process unrolls. The prosecutors I have met so far are sharp thinkers and dressers; they hang back and take in the big picture, then swoop down raptorlike to grab some tiny detail scuttling like a mouse in the dirt, and climb back to the stratosphere to digest. You wonder why such sharp guys are not working on Wall Street or defending up-market criminals at a million bucks an hour, but presumably a hawk would feel silly dressing up like a chicken and clucking even if there were money in it. Or maybe they are all running for something. Anyway, they're sharp.

I have always believed in the death penalty for murderers, and I still do.

The issue to my mind is how soon we forget the dead, assuming they are merely our fellow citizens—no more than that. It's hard for us to go on caring beyond a day or two, maybe a few weeks at the outside. But we show our respect for the dead, and proclaim the value of human life, by taking the trouble to execute murderers. Granted it's a terrific bother. Symbolism means nothing to us, we just barely comprehend it; ceremonial means nothing to us, and to go through a symbolic, ritual act that proclaims "this community condemns and will not tolerate murder"—a gruesome act that turns the stomach, when we have basically forgotten the reason—for us is hard. We'd a hell of a lot rather not bother. And *vengeance?* The families are chained down with grief forever. "Pain, pain ever, forever." If an execution relieves them even in the slightest, and I think it does, then we ought to do it—and if you want to call that vengeance, fine. I call it plain decency. Another word for it is justice.

Here is a man who murdered three people in the most cowardly way conceivable. His life's work was to take the nation by the collar and spit in its face. What's your most basic moral teaching, he asked us—not to murder? The hell with you; I flick away lives the way you flick ants off a picnic table. If out-raged justice doesn't grab us like a fist from the inside and *force* us to kill a man like that we might as well face it, the dignity of human life means nothing to us any more; it means nothing; zero. We are only going through the motions of justice, reading a script from a book, mouthing the words, comprehending nothing.

I would sentence him to death. And I would commute the sentence in one case only, if he repents, apologizes and begs for-giveness of the dead men's families, and the whole world—and tells us how he plans to spend the whole rest of his life pleading with us to hate the vileness and evil he embodied and to love life, to protect and defend it, and tells us how he sees with per-fect agonizing clarity that he *deserves* to die—then and only then I'd commute his sentence; not on the grounds that his lawyers slithered through some hole or other.

My own injuries don't constitute a capital crime. For what he did to me, I wouldn't dirty my mind thinking about him. For what he could have done to my boys and my wife I would strangle him with my bare hands, if I had the hands left. If someone handed me a gun or showed me the switch on the chair, I would kill him myself. (People will quote me out of context—but only fools; the hell with them.)

And if he repents? Spends the rest of his days pleading with the world to hate evil, to hate what he stood for and what he did? Then yes, I would relent and commute his sentence. I would have to.

CHAPTER NINE

H OW DID IT HAPPEN? Did an "intellectualized class" overwhelm the old business-and-upper class, as the New Class theorists had it? Or was the outcome decided by a bloodless coup in the generals' tent, within the tiny upper stratum that calls the shots and sets the tone?

No doubt there was a big engagement in the field—but a takeover at the top was decisive.

Consider that the top-level, elite positions themselves haven't changed much. Top politicians and their staffers, judges and top lawyers, leading bureaucrats and business and financial and newspaper and entertainment people, prominent clergymen and academics—they were the big cheeses of 1930 and 1960 and, with an adjustment here and there (entertainers up, clergymen down), they still are. And the supply lines that feed these positions are the same, anyway in one key respect. *The prestige colleges play a central role in staffing the elite.* They did in 1930 and 1960 and still do—the Princetons and Harvards,

Dukes and Stanfords, Georgetowns and Amhersts. A 1990 *Fortune* magazine survey of CEOs at Fortune 500 companies found, for example, that "the dominance of the Ivy League is, if anything, increasing: Whereas 14% of the former CEOs surveyed hold Ivy League degrees, nearly 19% of the current CEOs do." Yale ranked first as a CEO-supplier, Princeton second. Of the eight Presidents since 1961, half are Ivy League products one way or another: Kennedy from Harvard, Bush from Yale, Ford and Clinton from Yale Law. I could go on, but the point is obvious—students and parents who pay fabulous sums for prestige degrees have their reasons, and quality of teaching is not exactly the whole story. Loads of important people graduate from unprestigious colleges or none, that goes without saying. College training barely matters at all to our brightest lights; it beads up and rolls right off. But the top colleges swing a lot of weight today, as they did in 1960 and 1930 too. Make big changes to these institutions and big changes in the American elite *must* follow.

And big changes were made, great big ones. Starting in the late '40s, admission and hiring policies were transformed; broadly speaking, intellectuals took over the faculty and the student bodies. I mean "took over" in the sense of progressing not from zero influence to complete control, but from a subordinate to a dominating position.

The universities had always harbored *some* intellectuals, but Harvard or Princeton students used to be mainly the richest, not the smartest; on the faculty, social connections used to be as good a criterion for tenure as any; the Yale man and Vassar girl were social types, not incipient intellectuals. The goal at the fancy colleges used to be *to civilize* well-off young gentlemen and ladies, which involved a certain amount of teaching and a large amount of socializing, domesticating and attitude-inculcating. From a 1941 Yale alumni handbook (the citations in this paragraph come from Dan Oren's *Joining the Club* of 1985): "It is generally assumed that, even with a scholarship, the poor boy entering Yale will be handicapped socially unless he happens to be an athletic star. He is assumed to have no chance to compete successfully with the graduates of Eastern preparatory schools for anything except scholastic honors." *Wrong!* "Yale will polish rough exteriors." Yale is in the polishing business. "What I want for Yale college," the Dean wrote in a 1948 report to the President, "is an intellectual eminence as great as her athletic or her social or her eminence in activities of all sorts." (He notes also that "the rewards which American society offers to brains are meagre.") Things moved briskly in the Dean's direction. One dramatic sign was the big influx of Jews; the intellectualizing trend went a lot farther than bringing in Jews, of course, but Jews are a dye marker that allows us to trace a new class of people as it moves into the system—a class distinguished by intellect, not social standing. At the prestige colleges today the goal is to *intellectualize:* to inculcate the intellectual's habits, not the lady's or gentleman's.

The revolution that changed America was no conspiracy. It was a tragedy, created by noble intentions and good deeds that, whatever their consequences, neither can nor ought to be undone.

The old elite made the revolution itself; kicked it off by volunteering to make room for a new class. Nothing compelled the Harvards and Yales to change their ways. They did it on their own. The rise of the intellectualized elite is connected, in this view, to the retreat of the deeply shaken upper classes worldwide after World War II. Today's American culture was shaped ultimately by the same forces that made Europe abandon Empire—in some cases under the gun, but in other important ones because the will to rule was gone. Richard Brookhiser writes something similar in *The Way of the WASP:* "In their guilt, WASPs not only do the right thing by those who wish to become WASPs, but they extend themselves for the benefit of those who intend to remain something else."

Pretend that the only history you know is the postwar transformation of the prestige colleges. What predictions would you make? The faculty transformation picks up steam throughout the 1950s. By the early '60s it is largely complete: Intellectual rigor and distinction are the main hiring criteria now, and young professors are increasingly apt to be card-carrying intellectuals. Students matriculating in the early '60s are the first who will get the full treatment. Would-be intellectuals are increasingly prominent in the student bodies also. The first of the new breed ought to be done and pop out of college somewhere (check your watches) in the mid-'60s, out of graduate and professional schools starting in the late '60s. In the late 1960s a period of strife should begin inside the elite, but chances are it won't be long before the old guard calls a retreat and the young guard takes over. After all, this is the same old guard that remade the colleges. It has been turning itself out to pasture for years. In this reading, our national turmoil over Vietnam was a symptom and not the disease, embittering a transformation that was in the cards anyway.

———

Let's say there *was* a coup at the top; that, after the war, intellectuals took the helm at the prestige colleges, that a new breed of intellectualized graduates duly emerged to claim (as these graduates always had) a large share of the nation's elite positions; that the character of the elite changed radically in consequence. Today's elite is intellectualized, the old elite was not—but why should that matter? What differences does it make?

The difference is this: The old elite got on fairly well with the nation it was set over. But the enmity between Intellectual and Bourgeois is sheepman against cattleman, farm against city, Army versus Navy: a cliché but real. Ever since there *was* a middle class, intellectuals have despised it. When intellectuals were outsiders, their loves and hates never mattered much. But today they are running things, and their tastes matter greatly.

Members of the old social upper-crust elite were richer and better educated than the public at large, but they approached life on basically the same terms. The public went to church and so did they. The public went into the army and so did they. The public staged simpler weddings and the elite put on fancier ones, but they mostly all used the same dignified words and no one self-expressed. They agreed (this being America) that art was a waste, scientists were questionable, engineering and machines and progress and nature were good—some of the old-time attitudes made sense and some didn't, but the staff and the bosses were basically in accord. (George Bush was elected in part, Brookhiser suggests, because of public interest in restoring the old arrangements.)

Today's elite loathes the public. Nothing personal, just a fundamental difference in world view, but the hatred is unmistakable. Occasionally it escapes in scorching geysers. Michael Lewis reports in *The New Republic* on the '96 Dole presidential campaign: "The crowds flip the finger at the busloads of journalists and chant rude things at them as they enter each arena. The journalists, for their part, wear buttons that say 'Yeah, I'm the Media. Screw You.'" The crowd hates the reporters, the reporters hate the crowd—an even matchup, except that the reporters wield power and the crowd (in effect) wields none. The Virginia Military Institute used to be male-only. The elite didn't like that, and set to work. Thus Geoffrey Norman in the *American Spectator:* "A *Washington Post* columnist wrote that VMI existed in a 'medieval time warp, in which brotherhood is forged through sado-masochistic rituals in a forgotten monastery supported by the state for its own Byzantine purposes.' A state senator from Virginia notified the world that she had 'trouble with young men who want to shave their heads and shower together.'" The elite hated VMI, and no doubt VMI hated the elite—another even matchup, except that, when it occurred to the elite one afternoon on the way to the water cooler that VMI's way of life ought to be wiped out (just a casual notion, inasmuch as the likes of VMI hardly matter to the elite one way or the other), it was duly wiped out. The old regime was crushed like a beer can under a tank tread and the Institute is now, needless to say, coed. Having put things right and fundamentally refashioned the quirky, proud old college, the elite is unlikely to think about it again for the next hundred years. Again, this is no conspiracy; the lawyers who argued for the Justice Department, the reporters who covered the case and the Supreme Court majority that decided it all just happened to see eye-to-eye with the intelligentsia.

A vignette of opposed world views: In 1994 a tattoo artist in Columbus, Ohio named Adam Gray refused to bestow his art on a would-be customer who had AIDS. Gray offered to do him a skin-painting instead, but the customer insisted on the needle—and appealed, when Gray refused, to the Ohio Civil Rights Commission. The commissioners ordered Gray to fork over some cash so the AIDS patient could get a tattoo elsewhere, to post a sign confessing to an act of discrimination and to sign a gag order forbidding him to discuss the case. Gray refused. The commissioners mulled it over for two years more, then ordered Gray to pick up his needle and give the man a tattoo—either that or give some other AIDS patient a tattoo. And Gray was never again to turn away an AIDS-infected customer. Gray launched another appeal. He has shelled out fifty thousand in legal fees so far.

To the Civil Rights Commissioners ideas are the main thing, and universal tolerance is their favorite. The commissioners are part of the intellectualized elite. Tattoo artists are not, and the case is defined for Adam Gray (you have to guess) not by a clash of ideas but a mere fact, the fact that a man who comes into contact with AIDS-infected blood can get AIDS and die. Of course you might claim that this disagreement simply pits one idea against another, Gray's idea being that a man should avoid doing things that might kill him. But there is a crucial distinction between propositions you arrive at by reasoning (such as universal tolerance) and ones that are based on emotion or experience or horse sense. The Talmud calls this elusive stuff *derekh eretz,* literally "way of the world"—a phrase that also means "deference" or "humility." One of the Talmud's deepest assertions is also one of its simplest: *yafeh talmud Torah im derekh eretz,* Torah study *together with* worldly experience is beautiful. Ideas against a background of humility and common sense. (Some of the greatest Talmudic thinkers didn't earn their living as rabbis; they were shoemakers, merchants, carpenters.)

A judge in Philadelphia named Norma Shapiro orders the mass release of criminals and dangerous defendants from city jails. She is part of the intellectualized elite, where ideas are the main thing, and humane treatment of prisoners is another favorite. Thousands of those released prisoners are subsequently rearrested for cause, charged during one eighteen-month period with 90 rapes and 79 murders. One lucky recipient of a Norma Shapiro get-out-of-jail-free card murders in cold blood a young policeman named Danny Boyle. In the anger of Boyle's family and friends and the Philadelphians who grieve with them, you see not a policy disagreement but a class conflict. The idea class, the power-over-prisoners class, the intellectualized elite is opposed by a different class for whom ideas are no good at best unless you mix them with experience, common sense, humanity, humility, *derekh eretz.* "It is always sobering," E. B. White writes in a 1942 letter inspired by a brush with FDR's high-toned advisers, "to encounter the intellectual idealists at work, for they seem to live in a realm of their own, making their plans for the world in much the same way that any common tyrant does." Thus Simone de Beauvoir, the type of an intellectual idealist, in *The Second Sex* (cited again by Graglia): "No woman should be authorized to stay at home to raise her children. . . . Women should not have that choice, precisely because if there is such a choice, too many women will make that one." Simone, meet Norma. "Common tyrant" is the phrase White used.

The nation today is captured perfectly in a *New Republic* cartoon. (*The New Republic* is the conscience of liberalism, and the cartoon is unrepresentative of the magazine, but it *is* representative of something bigger.) The first three panels show a white male whining about Affirmative Action, presumably having become a target himself. "Affirmative Action has left a bitter taste," he says. "It's nothing more than discrimination, and discrimination of *any* kind is wrong. People should be judged by what they can do, not what group they're part of." In the last panel we get an explanation for his heartfelt stand against bigotry: a bottle and a spoon, with a label on the bottle reading "Affirmative Action—A Taste of His Own Medicine."

(As if he used to be in the habit of pummeling people; we start pummeling him and he tells us "Stop!—I see at last that pummeling people is wrong!") Over the bottle the cartoonist has written his laconic verdict on the "affirmative action" treatment: "Seems to have worked."

It is amazing how much the cartoonist has unwittingly let slip about the elite and its world view. Our whining white male didn't prescribe this medicine for *himself.* Patients don't do that. We prescribed it *for* him. We doctors, we the elite. We who know better. He was sick and we cured him. Intellectuals going back a century and more have had lots of prescriptions in store for the obstinate, dimwitted public. Many medicines awaiting deployment.

A spring '97 article in *The New York Times* asked whether liberal supporters of traditional welfare hadn't brought the 1996 Welfare Reform Act on themselves, at least in part, by ignoring the public's gathering outrage. But the fact is, one elitenik explained, supporters of old-style welfare felt that they couldn't talk frankly about its problems, because to do so would "just encourage people to cut, slash and burn." This observation makes sense only in light of two underlying assumptions: (1) If we tell "people" the truth, they will react with their usual gross robot stupidity. But (2) if we don't tell them, we are in the clear. Surely they are too dumb to find out for themselves.

In these paragraphs I am reading a political cartoon and a snippet from a news article more closely than you ordinarily would. But I stand by this textual or literary-critical or close-reading approach to modern society, and the assumptions that emerge strike me as worth pondering.

Does the public hate the elite back? Surveys suggest that it disdains journalists and politicians, and an especially jarring one showed, not long ago, that the only career parents would choose less happily for their children than "President of the United States" is "movie star." (In 1986, the year before he died, someone noticed Fred Astaire at a restaurant in Hollywood and word got around among the customers. No one bothered him, but when he got up to leave, the entire establishment applauded as he walked to the door. It is hard to grasp nowadays, but people admired Astaire not only as an artist and performer but as a gentleman.) Yet President Clinton is *the* paradigm intellectualized-elitenik, and a public that elected him twice could hardly be eaten up by class hatred (which is, it hardly needs saying, a damned good thing).

The public's political preferences have drifted rightward in recent years, yet in the last few decades they have been remarkably stable overall. Which signifies acceptance of the new order, or at least resignation? Maybe. But notice how little is at stake in a typical election on basic cultural grounds. Republicans and Democrats stand for different policies. But an American Middle East–watcher made a fascinating comment, years ago, about the Islamic revolution in Iran: To the Iranians, he said, Americans and Soviets looked pretty much the same. There were big philosophical differences between them, but they all wore pants. Orthodox Islam peels away from the West closer to the ground than the point where communism and democratic capitalism branch apart. The divide between the elite and the public might likewise be more basic than Republican–Democrat differences. Leading Republicans speak the elite's language just as the Democrats do ("Diversity is our strength"—Newt Gingrich), honor and obey the basic tenets of orthodox feminism, are no more inclined than Democrats to be hemmed in by traditional family structure. When VMI's future was on the line, you didn't see Republicans rallying to its side. A few complained; most shrugged. At their 1996 Convention, Republicans lavished attention on AIDS victims and rape victims, former welfare mothers and powerful female politicans—God bless 'em every one, but in cultural terms the Democrats and Republicans are all wearing pants.

So, the Canonical American is dead. The nation's two major groups don't like each other; they admire different qualities and personalities. Citizenship doesn't swing much weight any more. With no Canonical American, it is a hard concept even to grasp.

Is there anything to be done? Of course. And of course, it won't happen because I say it should—but I lay this out not as a set of clothes I expect society to hop right into, but as a prediction of what you will see it wearing when it finally decides to change its ridiculous outfit.

If you don't spend your time providing objects or services of practical use, if instead you turn out ideas, thoughts, visions, inspirations, art objects and whatnot that matter only to the mind and spirit, then you are a thinker. (This definition is unclear in a dozen ways, but for my purposes, pinning it down doesn't buy anything. A rough definition is enough, and the discussion that follows is only a sketch.) We have the idea nowadays that if you are a thinker, you belong in the cultural group we call "intellectuals." "Thinker" is like "broccoli farmer" in that it describes how you spend your time. "Intellectual" is something like "conservative"; it refers to a certain clump of attitudes and interests. People in the "intellectual" clump don't all share one outlook, any more than "conservatives" do. But on the whole they have enough in common to make the group name useful.

Some people insist that "intellectual" is just a job category, or only means that you have a certain type of education. But everyone knows that intellectuals aren't crazy about Winnebagos. Everyone knows that they are more likely to go to a ballet than a tractor pull. Those facts have no real connection to a person's degree of learning or what he does for a living. Where males are concerned, for example, ballet makes a far more direct appeal than tractor pulls, centering as it does on flocks of young women, many of them (albeit in a tubercular way) good-looking, moving gracefully in short skirts. Any heterosexual male can see the point of that, whereas a tractor pull means nothing unless you're up on the arcane rules, the types of engine, tires, suspension and whatnot. But intellectuals have definite tastes and tendencies.

(I discussed some of those tastes and tendencies earlier, and the ones I mentioned are usually classified "liberal" or "left," but of course there are conservative intellectuals also. Nevertheless, while there have always been black sheep and conservative intellectuals, the average sheep is white and the average intellectual is left. I myself am a lot fonder of the blacks, but I have to face facts. They are, always were and are likely to remain a small minority.)

It used to be that the "thinker" category was associated with two cultural groups, not one; there were intellectual thinkers and nonintellectual thinkers. You might call the two groups high-church and low-church, where "high-church" corresponds to the intelligentsia as it is today. The low-church group has disappeared; individual specimens still exist, but the group has disbanded.

Nowadays the whole idea of a "nonintellectual thinker" strikes people as odd, but low-church thinkers had their own distinct cultural profile. They tended to discount ideology and be infatuated with technique. Humor was basic to their world view. They prided themselves on skepticism and impiety but favored conventional family arrangements. They often boasted of worldliness. They wrote seriously about sports long before intellectuals took up the topic. They disliked abstraction and were gluttons for nitty-gritty detail about the look, sound, smell, taste and feel of everything around them. They celebrated their attachments to their hometowns and native landscapes. Obviously you couldn't count on all these characteristics showing up in any particular low-church specimen, and the border between low church and high was never sharply drawn. But people knew the border existed, and it was important to U.S. culture. Intellectuals stood for a certain approach to life, and this other group stood for a different one.

In 1940 many reporters and newspaper editors were low-church thinkers. (Others, then as now, weren't thinkers at all.) Certain writers, industrial artists and designers, theater and pop music and entertainment and publishing industry people were low-church. Many high-church types were professors or were associated with high-toned journals or magazines. There were artists in both camps. Low-church artists were famous or notorious with the public. High-church types played mainly to intellectuals and other artists. (High-church, intellectual artists were men like Duchamp in his post-painter stage, or the composers Schoenberg and Ives, or the architects Gropius and Mies van der Rohe—as opposed to a Wright or a Hood or a James Gamble Rogers.)

Low-church thinkers used to be *the* characteristic American (versus European) type. They used to be the cultural essence of New York as opposed to Paris. They were overwhelmed as a group by the same wave that swept the intelligentsia into power: Two parties were reduced to one. Nowadays most work-

ers in the traditional low-church trades are under the intellectuals' sway: the reporters and non-hack popular writers, the
scriptwriters and movie producers, the designers, editors,
thoughtful businessmen.

Who were the members of the defunct low-church band?
Take the great painter Stuart Davis. He laid out once in concrete detail the "things which have made me want to paint,
outside of other paintings":

> American wood and iron work of the past; Civil War and
> skyscraper architecture; the brilliant colors on gasoline
> stations, chainstore fronts, and taxi-cabs; the music of
> Bach; synthetic chemistry; the poetry of Rimbaud; fast
> travel by train, auto, and aeroplane which brought new
> and multiple perspectives; electric signs; the landscape
> and boats of Gloucester, Mass.; 5 & 10 cent store kitchen
> utensils; movies and radio; Earl Hines hot piano and Ne-
> gro jazz music in general, etc.

The eminent writer Joseph Mitchell is the essence of the low-
church man. (You could argue that he was the greatest writer in
the United States when he died in 1996, although for reasons
unknown he hadn't published a thing in thirty-two years.) His
pieces are so packed with detail, they sometimes come off as all
filling and no crust; unlike such distinguished low-church colleagues as A. J. Liebling and E. B. White, Mitchell rarely pauses
even to wisecrack. "There are clams on the sludgy bottom, and
mussels and mud shrimp and conchs and crabs and sea worms
and sea plants." "He has an old-Roman face. It is strong-jawed
and prominent-nosed and busy-eyebrowed and friendly and
reasonable and sagacious and elusively piratical." He cares little
for conventional writerly frameworks. When he has said

enough, he stops on an interesting detail like a driver veering into the first parking space he can find. But his eye is so sharp, his prose so precise and his fascination with these details and the people telling them is so warm and deep, his pieces are compelling no matter what the topic.

In his essay about McSorley's, Mitchell tells us that Stuart Davis used to be a regular patron—also John Sloan and George Luks. "They were all good painters," he says, "and didn't put on airs, and the workingmen in the saloon accepted them as equals." Low-church thinkers weren't necessary convivial regular guys (Edward Hopper wasn't); they were just as likely to be recluses. But they were certainly no less learned than intellectuals. Hopper once took his future wife on a date and, discovering she spoke French, recited to her the opening of a Verlaine poem he loved. When he stopped, she took it up and recited the rest. They were low-church types, not intellectuals: "Mr. Hopper has never joined a cause," an art critic wrote in 1924, "nor been the exponent of a theory." Love of poetry and knowledge of Verlaine don't make you an intellectual.

In the days of Harold Ross (from '25 through '51), the *New Yorker* was the quintessential low-church publication: infatuated with technique, humor and the concrete detail, not interested in ideology, professors, politics or theory. Which isn't surprising, since Ross himself was an "anti-intellectual"—that's what the literary critic Edmund Wilson called him, and Ross's biographer Thomas Kunkel agrees. (Ross hired Wilson and clearly tolerated intellectuals to a point, but only when there was nothing better at hand.) E. B. White represented Ross's *New Yorker* at its best. White was in no way typical of anything. He even launched an occasional ideological crusade; when he was on his world-government kick, during and after World War II, you might almost have taken him for an intellectual.

Or maybe low-church thinkers *do* launch ideological crusades at times, but only when they are desperate. In any case, White had no interest in trading opinions with the intelligentsia. He wanted to doctor his pig, fish with his son and chat with his wife. And sometimes write.

The collapse of the two-party system in American thinkerdom had dramatic consequences. Consider the newspapers. The press used to be mainly Republican; it was a constant nuisance to FDR during the New Deal. Today it is mainly Democratic—as you can see in many ways, for example in a recent survey of the Washington press corps, which voted overwhelmingly for Clinton over Bush in 1992. Reporters are entitled to their opinions and might as well be left-leaning as right-leaning; it makes no difference in principle. The intelligentsia on the other hand was left-leaning in the New Deal and still is. What's noteworthy is not that the press leans left, but the way it has swung around and aligned itself with the intellectualized elite. Of course today all aspiring reporters go to college, and newspapers hire journalism school graduates. In 1940 some reporters had college degrees, but plenty didn't. Journalism school was a fairly new idea, and the newspaper industry was lukewarm. Stanley Walker put it this way when he was city editor of the *Herald Tribune* in 1934: "Virtually all of the graduates have a ready, workmanlike style, but something, somewhere, seems to have happened to them. Is it because so many of their teachers never were very great shakes as newspaper men?"

Consider the art world. It changed dramatically as the low church disappeared and the intellectuals took over. It is hard to believe today, but there used to be a strong connection between contemporary artists and the public. The public knew what was going on in the art world. It reacted ordinarily with jokes and scorn, but mocking implies interest. The popular press joked about cubism, surrealism, abstract sculpture, abstract painting, pop art. After the 1960s the jokes tailed off—not because public taste got more sophisticated; because people no longer gave a damn.

The public didn't withdraw from art so much as art withdrew from the public. Artists enrolled en masse in the intelligentsia, and most of them, nowadays, aim their productions strictly at other intellectuals. Dislike of the middle class was always widespread among artists, but nowadays it has turned humorless and vicious. (Here is a representative example, a work by Frank Moore—born in New York, 1953—that was selected for the Whitney Museum's 1995 Biennial. It's a parody of Norman Rockwell's famous Thanksgiving illustration "Freedom from Want"; Moore shows whites, blacks and Asians around a festive table as the mother, who is white, presents a parsley-decorated platter of drugs and syringes in a turkey-shaped heap.) No cultural sphere is more thoroughly intellectualized than art. "Conceptual art" is big, along with arcane pieces of all sorts that are intended merely to communicate ideas obtusely. It's no accident that words have become such important elements in contemporary painting. Nowhere are aesthetic qualities in general, or beauty in particular, spoken of with more contempt than in today's art world. Art schools used to teach technique; nowadays the prestigious ones despise it. And in politics, the contemporary artist's agenda just happens to line up beautifully with the intelligentsia's. "While I am a socialist," said John Sloan around the turn of the twentieth century, "I never allowed social propaganda to get into my paintings." If you imagine reading that statement to a modern artist-intellectual, you can't help picturing his dumbfoundedness—the giant car-

toon question mark materializing over his head. (But isn't social propaganda the whole *point?* How can you make art that
isn't socially aware?)

You still do find thinkers here and there with the old low-
church proclivities. But they are isolated specimens and not the
breeding colony they used to be. A few are important but they
have no influence as a group. When the low church went out of
business, the intelligentsia picked up a few of its characteristics.
Sports are fashionable with intellectuals nowadays but didn't
used to be. The same holds for nature, and high-class food and
wine. The intelligentsia seems to have acquired these traits the
way a triumphant business hires a few of the dead competitor's
star workers. But the high church remains true to its big prin-
ciples.

If the low church used to be so prominent in American culture, how come it never even had a name? Isn't that somewhat
fishy? A person bumps into a lot of things that ought to have
names and don't; nevertheless, it is somewhat fishy. But I'd
guess that the group never acquired a name because its members blended seamlessly with the country at large.

Intellectuals hold themselves aloof. When they mix with the
masses—out of sincere interest at times, and with the best intentions—their self-consciousness surrounds them like a Secret
Service escort. ("So Robert Lowell and Norman Mailer feigned
deep conversation"—Mailer is describing a Washington party
where he and Lowell, being the biggest celebrities in attendance, had naturally gone off by themselves. "They turned
their heads to one another at the empty table, ignoring the po-
tentially acolytic drinkers at either elbow." Gelernter confesses
for his part that he is a big admirer of Lowell's poetry and some
of Mailer's prose, and it was not for too little that Gelernter had

published a review praising Mailer's widely panned book about Picasso, although he despised nearly everything Mailer stood for except a sharp eye and good writing.)

Low-church thinkers took a different approach. Look at John Sloan or Stuart Davis at McSorley's and you can't miss the naturalness of their intentions. They want to drink with the others. E. B. White in that small Maine town of his, Ross losing a bundle at poker, Liebling at a boxing match, Mitchell kibbitzing with the proprietor at Sloppy Louie's restaurant near the Fulton Fish Market—they seem at home and they are.

At the death of the celebrated *San Francisco Chronicle* columnist Herbert Caen, William Powers described in *The New Republic* the newspaper culture of half a century ago: "Young reporters didn't repair after work to the health club and the first available Stairmaster; they bowled with small-time vaudeville performers. The writing of Caen and reporters of his breed reflected the city life in which they were then immersed." During World War II and Korea, American reporters mixed with the troops and on occasion risked their necks to help out. They didn't fret (as elite TV newsreaders do today) about seeming "too partisan." Of course they were partisan. Joseph Cornell was a towering master of twentieth century art. Strolling down Main Street in Flushing, Queens, doing errands and having meals and (in his diffident way) chatting up the shopgirls at Woolworth's, Bickford's, Nedick's and Chock Full o' Nuts, he was happy and at ease and at home.

The uneasiness I've always suffered about my own role in life comes, in part, from the fact that I was cut out to be a low-church thinker, but the church had been abolished when the time arrived to join. So I signed up (so to speak) with the con-

servative intellectuals instead. I like and admire these people
and am proud to be associated with them.

But in some respects I am not one of them—being, in some
respects, not an intellectual at all. I would sell out their entire
economic program—would double taxes, quintuple government spending—if it would buy me a modicum of national
support for a politics-free English language. When the language goes down the drain, you lose everything. I would give
up the White House for a generation in exchange for a major
national newspaper that was dedicated to good writing and
nonideological reporting, covered art in depth from the standpoint of art and not politics, didn't confuse "objectivity" with
evenhandedness as between good and evil. Much as I admire
conservative intellectuals, I think they are too willing to address politicians and each other instead of the public. And they
care far more about politics, government and economics than I
could ever manage to.

It all comes down to the same thing in the end: I'm a misfit
from any angle. In some ways I am an intellectual. I have an intellectual's tendency to make up theories; I not only work at
Yale, I'm deeply attached to the place. On top of which, I own
a goddamned Volvo. My credentials as a *non*-intellectual are
recorded in dozens of strange incidents over the years, my al-
bum of oddities. Here's one little specimen: I've mentioned
that my master plan called for no art courses in college. The
same held for writing and literature—writing being the other
thing I was completely engrossed in, and certain I could do
well; so I didn't take a single English course either. I was per-
versely determined to avoid a college education in exactly those
topics I cared about most. The same for high school, to the extend I could manage it.

In high school I was happy to do right by the up-market science, math and history sequences but refused to go into advanced English, which every non-nitwit was expected to attend. English was required, so I enrolled in the standard sequence (and incidentally had some first-rate teachers). My wrong attitude was noted. But it didn't matter until a teachers' committee appointed me official school representative (or one of them, there may have been several) to an all-county (or all-something) student-writers' fest. At that point the big guns of the English department opened fire, and I came under high-caliber disapproval—which, of course, I ignored. It's not as if my prose was any good. It was like my poetry: If you read it aloud in a good clear voice with meticulous enunciation, you could kill a man at fifty paces.

I would hardly have called it a "budding aversion to the intelligentsia" at the time, but it was. Of course if I had wanted to steer *way* clear, I could have shipped out by tramp freighter for malarial foreign ports and nurtured my prose style in more colorful surroundings than a Yale dorm room. But I didn't. Confused as I was, it was all I could do to put one foot after the other and march forward in the direction momentum and official approval carried me.

As a nation we have reestablished all sorts of temporarily absent species in the wild, and nothing would do us more good than to reestablish the low-church thinkers. The culture of the universities is set for a long time, and we can't change it. But we could establish new institutions with marked enough personalities to override it, to plunge their fresh hires into a culture radically different from the one they are used to. For the new hires it would be an ocean dive on a brisk day. Wakes a person up; you feel good afterward. (Allegedly.)

We could establish—or take over and rebuild—newspapers and news magazines, radio stations and TV production companies and museums and movie studios and theaters. The new institutions wouldn't be right-wing, but wouldn't be left-wing either. They would hire feminists and environmentalists, but not on the assumption that feminism and environmentalism are self-evidently correct. They would offer the same deal to antifeminists and anti-environmentalists. They would wash the accumulated dirt of elite politics and preaching and posing and bossing-around off U.S. culture the way you wash nine layers of grime off a beautiful, filthy car. They would be fanatic for technique, would insist that their writers must above all write well and their painters paint well. They would be capable of looking us square in the face and saying "the goal of art is beauty and truth" without snickering. They would hire and promote on merit. They would speak English properly. They would teach history honestly. They would spare us any pathetic, patronizing assertions that the foundation of American government and society is other than white, European and Christian. They would reject "multiculturalism" as a lie and a fraud. The wonderful thing about America, they would point out, isn't the chance it offered Jews (for example) to build *Jewish* culture—Jewish culture, you could argue, thrived better in the anti-Semitic ratholes of Poland and Lithuania than anywhere else in history. By all means let Jewish culture thrive everywhere, but the wonderful thing about America is the chance it offered all comers to build *American* culture, a plywood culture that gained strength from the crosswise grains of many separate, glued-up sheets.

I have to concede that, nowadays, most Americans would call this a far-right program. I think of it as completely apolitical—not left, not right, not center. "Hire and promote on merit" would have been just as incendiary in 1940 as it is today, but aside from that the whole agenda would have been filed under "motherhood and apple pie," once upon a time. Motherhood would have been filed there too.

Some people believe that proposals like this are good in principle; some people think they are cracked. Everyone agrees they are impossible. The logistic problems are stupendous, overwhelming. I admit it; no doubt they *are* impossible. But when I hear these objections, I can't help but think of E. B. White writing his publisher in 1958, in the course of revising William Strunk's *Elements of Style*.

> I cannot, and will-shall not, attempt to adjust the unadjustable Mr. Strunk to the modern liberal of the English Department, the anything-goes fellow. . . . I am against him, temperamentally and because I have seen the work of *his* disciples, and I say the hell with him.

Is the cause of good writing lost, now that academia has dropped it? "To me," White says—Mr. Practical—"no cause is lost." The chances of our repairing American culture might be zero. But I find it inspiring anyway that I can address the direct descendent of the anything-goes fellow, the intellectual who commands modern culture, in White's voice. I am against him. I have seen the work of his disciples, and I say the hell with him. To me no cause is lost.

CHAPTER TEN

Anyway, I now have a thumbpiece that works, here in 1997, and wear it much of the time. It's uncomfortable but tolerable. I take it off to type. I wear normal clothes. I can write decently left-handed. Writing takes more control than drawing—you can scale up a drawing to a size where your control is sure, but written letters usually have to be small. I remind myself as I write to hook my hand over and around in that strange left-handed way. The hook maneuver is guaranteed to smear your previous lines, but you can't work up any momentum otherwise: You write one letter and your hand just sits there. You shove it forward, write another and repeat. When I am sick of left-handedness I switch over to my right, if I am wearing the thumbpiece and glove, and lay down words as fast as I ever could, the only problem being that I can't exactly read them. But I can guess. Because my right-handed pen grip is so weak, the letters come out tumbling-drunk, unknotting themselves and falling over. In any case, I manage one way or another, and things are improving.

For a year or so after I was hurt, my arithmetic disappeared. I hate calculators and don't need or use them, but I do need to make notes except for short calculations. You can't calculate (except mentally) any faster than you can write numerals, and during that first year I could barely write them at all. They are loopier and more complicated than cursive letters. During my numeral-free year I couldn't take down phone numbers either. Someone might tell me over the phone "would you give him a call at . . . ," and a person feels damned silly saying "please repeat that slowly, because it takes me forty-five seconds to make an *8*." So I'd wind up with a bunch of gibberish and unfortunately I just couldn't make the call. This was my favorite symptom while it lasted.

My eye turned out to be a good candidate for a cornea transplant. Surgeons try to determine first whether the retina is in decent shape; no sense replacing the cornea if it isn't. It looked okay. But then the eye pressure was no good and had to be fixed. The operation came off. Finally a replacement cornea was installed. The surgeons were remarkably good, and the technology is amazing. My vision was much better afterward. But it turns out that the retina was damaged after all. Not as badly as it might have been, but some.

The great artist Edgar Degas was middle-aged when he first discovered that he could barely see out of one eye. I find such information far more interesting than I used to. I was never a great admirer of John Kennedy, but nowadays am inspired by the way he refused to let bouts of serious pain cramp his style. I had long admired Robert Dole but admire him more today, for his half-century of shrugging off injuries that in some ways resemble mine, but are in most respects much worse. I used to see Lord Halifax merely as Churchill's humdrum rival; I discovered not long ago that he had a wooden arm, and today I see him merely as Churchill's humdrum rival. Fellow-feeling has its limits. But I admire the way he carried off the wooden arm, the irrelevance to which he reduced it.

My right eye works a lot better than it did, but the blur in my vision still places between me and the world a gap that I suppose will always be there. I still do badly in crowds, but I never liked crowds anyway. Exhausted discomfort hits me in squalls now and then during the day; I flop down on my office sofa, if I can. For various reasons traveling is harder than it used to be, which has cost me money and (within computer science) a certain amount of professional standing. But no matter, I never liked traveling—not by myself, anyway.

I still take drugs for pain, for my right hand. It turns out that getting both sides of your hand lopped off feels exactly as you would expect it to. You don't get used to it, and the nerves sputter, boil and hiss on and on. But the situation has its ups and downs; there are times it drives me crazy, other times I don't notice it much. Various prescription drugs are useful. The pain could tail off and disappear some day.

Whether it does or not, what matters is that I can spend time as I always have with my family, can write and paint, can drive and play Legitimate Ball. That I have much to be grateful for is so obvious and so radically understates the case, it is barely even worth saying. But, what the hell—I have much to be grateful for. This is one reason the late Beethoven quartets had such a grip on me in the fall of '93, when I was coming around: The movement at the center of opus 132 called "Holy thanksgiving-song of a convalescent to the Godhead" is indeed holy. And the song has a middle section headed *Neue Kraft fühlend*, feeling new strength.

Having hopped with both feet into the careers I was intended for, painter and writer, but (with my customary decisiveness) having failed to give up my old career as technology professor, I am trapped in an unstable state. Something will have to change. "I do everything by halves," the artist Paul Klee once wrote—"art, making money, teaching, writing letters . . ." It's not the best way to live, but it's not the worst either.

It's starting to snow. Later I watch a cardinal in a snowy tree with my nine-year-old. He rarely has time for bird contemplation, given his busy schedule, the room-filling motorized structures he needs to assemble out of tiny plastic parts, the poems that need writing about his girlfriends. I'm afraid he is just as misaligned with the intellectual world's pat categories as I am. But at least he is a better engineer than I ever was, not to mention tap dancer, and maybe that will help. We are fifty feet away, and the cardinal is a bit of fluff in the distance, but we can't look away until it flies off in an awkward flurry. Three cardinals live nearby, two males and a female—skittish birds, all three suffering from permanent nervous breakdowns. They refuse to perch with the riffraff at a standard bird feeder; their contract stipulates that they will feed only while standing on the deck. We serve them specially purchased cardinal food (Purina Cardinal Chow, something like that, made up of equal parts hulled sunflower seeds and caviar), and when they deign to show up they are spectacular. For more information, refer to *Gelernter's Guide to the Birds of Southern New England and Their Mental Problems.*

So: What's the scoop on surviving a mail bomb? What do you learn? You learn that, at first, the past will seem only like a cause for mourning, but your job is to twist it around and make it a cause to rejoice. At the end of meals every Sabbath, observant Jews sing a psalm that has a strange muddle of verb tenses. Some scholars insist that the text is corrupt and propose changes, but only people who study the thing are confused; people who sing it understand. It begins with a story of the past. "When the Lord brought back the homecomers to Zion, we were like people who are dreaming . . ." A few verses later a prayer starts: "Restore our fortunes, Lord, like streams in the Negev"—which are dry all summer. Then the prayer breaks off, as if the author had suddenly changed his mind or remembered something, and the poem concludes with a series of flat assertions. "Those who sow in tears will reap shouting with joy! Weeping as he goes, he carries the seedbag—and returns with shouts of joy, carrying his sheaves." If you focus the big sweep of history on a single lifetime, the poet says, you see life as a stubborn return from sorrow again and again.

So your first task is to capture past and present and make them as firm underfoot as a concrete sidewalk. (The reason art exists.) Then you turn the past to advantage; go there as a refuge and use it to understand what is best in the present and what to do here.

And what emerges as most remarkable in the here-and-now is not the callousness or evil of the onslaught but the resilience of the defense. Only when the basics of culture and morality are under attack do we have the privilege of seeing their beauty (like stars when the city lights go dim) as clearly as we do today.

When the press is a roar of moral static, integrity in a journalist becomes remarkable. When it is perfectly okay for a

successful teacher to be a cant-spouting airhead, you understand properly what a serious teacher is worth. I'm not only
pleased, I'm moved when the rare student in one of my classes
hands me a paper that is defiantly bare of he-or-sheing and related stuff. A house with no propaganda posters means nothing
ordinarily, but if the authorities have decreed that every house
be plastered with propaganda posters. . . . It's a mark of our
own trendy, intellectual suburb and hundreds like it that my
wife came in smiling not long ago because she'd met a child
who addressed her as Mrs. and not by her first name. Around
here, the sweetest kids are raised rude as a matter of course (and
our own are no paragons), but when you meet one who is not,
it's uplifting. All sorts of simple courtesies that used to be automatic and largely meaningless are nowadays full of meaning,
signs of character and backbone, and the world is dense with
micro-miracles.

We used to live on a middle-class block in New Haven. In a
small house up the street was a couple who were both trained
as glaziers, but the wife quit when their child was born. Most
days, the husband drove long distances to reach some construction site where he could make a decent living. Their son
was our boy's first steady playmate. That woman walking down
the sidewalk past our front door pushing her stroller—not one
of those snazzy krypto-titanium jobs with damask upholstery
that the two-income families favored, just a stroller—was the
actual stuff of blessing, the physical embodiment of it, as portentous as any prophet's vision, here in our own time, in front
of our own noses. What the vision meant is that, when old age
shall this generation waste, long after the intellectuals are back
in their cages, the Victim Culture is gone, the arrogant bullying of today's elite is forgotten and the era of not knowing good
from evil is a distant memory, the mother's self-sacrificing love

for her child will endure as the picture of all love, all nobility and all blessing.

In the period after I was hurt, when perversity (despite the kindness of the people nearest by) beat down in torrents, I used the American past as a shelter. But you can't spend your life in that kind of shelter. In the end I had to come out. I often think that if I had lived sixty years ago, I would have been a Tin Pan Alley composer—but I might just as well have wound up as an unsuccessful herring dealer. Life was much harder for misfits back then. So I am back in the present. The only kind of shelter that holds up in the long term, under which you are allowed to hang around and (if need be) sulk forever, is the one represented by the canopy at a Jewish wedding, the home you make with your wife.

Our wedding ceremony was no more hitch-free than life in general. I wrote the music, for string quartet and flute; here is the Jane theme, for when the bride appears:

but the quartet we'd hired flubbed the all-important suspension one measure from the end, reducing the whole thing to rancid milk. (Naturally it had all gone perfectly in the run-through.) I was shocked when someone asked me right after the ceremony why, as the bride finished her approach and was coming in for a landing, I was scowling viciously. A ridiculous question. Hadn't everyone heard the wrong note? Things don't go exactly as you had hoped, but the bride was beautiful and I married her.

All is not for the best, and this is not the best of all possible worlds, but for me things have come out okay. The psalm is right: Life is a stubborn return from sorrow again and again. To suffer longing and loss makes you not a victim but a human being. And that sense of loss is your only real connection to human beings you don't like, to the ones with whom you disagree down to the ground. It is a subterranean connection, root-to-root; it connects you even, in the end, to your bitterest enemies.

On balance things have come out all right. "What Do Our Hearts Treasure?" is reprinted in White's *Collected Essays.* I have a paperback copy of the book beside me. It was in my office when the bomb went off, was soaked by the sprinkler and then freeze-dried and restored by the resourceful preservation office at the Yale library where the staff could reconstruct a melted Popsicle if you asked them to. It's too bad the book is bashed up. It reminds me of the explosion—but of course I wouldn't think of replacing it, because its departure and return were obviously intended to signify the link between White and me, his country and mine. A review by Jonathan Yardley is quoted on the back cover of the White book, and by a special one-time-only miracle, Yardley reviewed *1939* also and is quoted on the back of the paperback edition.

On balance things have come out all right. In our living-room is an old silver spice box, and my wife has put my wedding ring inside. She didn't tell me she had done it; one day I

just discovered it there. Spice boxes are used in a religious ceremony called *havdalah*, which closes the Sabbath at Saturday
sunset. You fill them with cloves, whose sweet scent conveys
your hope that the coming week won't be too bad, and consoles
you for the loss of the week and the Sabbath that are gone. The
box stands (in other words) for consolation and guarded hope.
We have several, and the one holding my ring was a tenth an-
niversary present from my wife. The cloves are still in it and are
still fragrant. I wish I could wear the ring; all is not for the best,
and I can't, but the spice box is the right place for it to stay.

NOTES

p. 3. According to E. B. White again in a different context: E. B. White, *One Man's Meat* (New York: Harper and Brothers, 1944), 254.

p. 11. By Robyn Gearey in *The New Republic:* "A Capital Crime," January 20, 1997, 12.

p. 11. Roughly half the murder cases in Los Angeles yield indictments: ibid.

p. 12. If thought corrupts language: George Orwell, "Politics and the English Language," in *A Collection of Essays* (New York: Doubleday Anchor, 1954), 174.

p. 18. James Thurber once said: James Thurber, *The Years with Ross* (Boston: Little, Brown, 1959), 66.

p. 61. Back in 1957, Norman Mailer: see Paul Johnson, *Intellectuals* (London: Weidenfeld and Nicolson, 1988), 322.

p. 61. Writes the film critic Stanley Kauffmann: "What's Left of the Center?" *Salmagundi, A Quarterly of the Humanities and Social Sciences,* no. 111, Summer 1996, 105–9.

p. 62. "The 1960s," historian Paul Johnson writes: Johnson, *Intellectuals,* 322.

p. 62. "The last time I visited New York," writes E. B. White: *Essays of E. B. White* (New York: Harper and Row, 1979), viii.

p. 65. Eudora Welty wrote, in her 1984 memoirs: *One Writer's Beginnings* (Cambridge, Mass.: Harvard University Press, 1984), 39.

p. 65. E. B. White in the final, 1979 edition: William Strunk and E. B. White, *The Elements of Style, Third Edition* (Boston: Allyn and Bacon, 1979), 60.

p. 65. When I write and the sound of it comes back to my ears: Welty, *One Writer's Beginnings,* 12.

p. 69. Marjorie Hillis says of New York: Marjorie Hillis, *New York, Fair or No Fair* (New York: Bobbs-Merrill, 1939), 12.

p. 69. According to the *Londoner's Guide to New York:* E. Stewart Fay, *Londoner's Guide to New York* (London: Methuen, 1936).

p. 90. Today roughly 1,200,000 school-age children are educated at home: see Michael Farris, "Solid Evidence to Support Home Schooling," *Wall Street Journal,* March 5, 1997, A18.

p. 105. Draggers, trawlers, mackerel seiners, and lobster boats: Joseph Mitchell, *Up in the Old Hotel* (New York: Pantheon Books, 1992), 539.

p. 108. What he did for entertainment as a boy was, the captain says: ibid., 548.

p. 126. Yale will polish rough exteriors: cited in Dan Oren, *Joining the Club: A History of Jews and Yale* (New Haven: Yale University Press, 1985), 174.

p. 126. The rewards which American society offers to brains: ibid., xiv.

p. 127. In their guilt, WASPs not only do the right thing: Richard Brookhiser, *The Way of the WASP* (New York: Free Press, 1991), 133.

p. 128. Michael Lewis reports in *The New Republic:* "The End," Nov. 25, 1996, 21.

p. 129. Geoffrey Norman in the *American Spectator:* "Crashing VMI's Line," Dec. 1996, 39.

p. 129. In 1994 a tattoo artist in Columbus, Ohio named Adam Gray: see "Tattoo You," *Heterodoxy,* Sept. 1996, 3.

p. 131. E. B. White writes in a 1942 letter: *Letters of E. B. White,* collected and edited by Dorothy L. Guth (New York: Harper and Row, 1976), 223.

p. 131. A *New Republic* cartoon: April 24, 1995.

p. 132. A spring '97 article in *The New York Times:* Kevin Sack, "Given Not an Inch, Political Foes Take a Mile," April 13, 1997, sec. 4, 1.

p. 137. Things which have made me want to paint: cited in Karen Wilkin, *Stuart Davis* (New York: Abbeville Press, 1987), 12.

p. 137. There are clams on the sludgy bottom: Mitchell, *Up in the Old Hotel,* 465; he has an old-Roman face: ibid., 587.

p. 138. They were all good painters: ibid., 12.

p. 138. Mr. Hopper has never joined a cause: cited in Gail Levin, *Edward Hopper: An Intimate Biography* (New York: Knopf, 1995), 187.

p. 139. Stanley Walker put it this way: *City Editor, 1934* (New York: Frederick A. Stokes, 1934).

p. 140. Said John Sloan around the turn of the twentieth century: cited in Rebecca Zurier, Robert W. Snyder and Virginia M. Mecklenburg, *Metropolitan Lives: The Ashcan Artists and Their New York* (New York: National Museum of American Art, 1995), 45.

p. 141. So Robert Lowell and Norman Mailer feigned deep conversation: Norman Mailer, *The Armies of the Night* (New York: New American Library, 1968), 18–19.

p. 142. At the death of the celebrated *San Francisco Chronicle* columnist Herbert Caen: William Powers, "Raising Caen," *New Republic,* May 12, 1997, 19.

p. 146. E. B. White writing his publisher in 1958: *Letters of E. B. White,* 455.